# Maritime Affairs

## Integrated Management for India

# Maritime Affairs

## Integrated Management for India


Commander Manoj Gupta



(Established: 1870)

United Service Institution of India
Admiral R D Katari Chair

Manas Publications
New Delhi-110002 (INDIA)

**MANAS PUBLICATIONS**
(Publishers, Distributors, Importers & Exporters)
4858, Prahlad Street,
24, Ansari Road, Darya Ganj,
New Delhi - 110 002 (INDIA)
**Ph.: 23260783, 23265523 (O); 27131660**
**Fax: 011-23272766**
**E-mail: manaspublications@vsnl.com**
**Web site: www.manaspublications.com**



First Published 2005

**ISBN** 81-7049-209-2
Rs 495/-



*Typeset at*
Manas Publications

*Printed in India at*
Nice Printing Press
and Published by Mrs Suman Lata for
**Manas Publications,** 4858, Prahlad Street,
24, Ansari Road, Darya Ganj,
New Delhi - 110 002 (INDIA)

**Dedicated to Gen-Next:**

Our children, Mihir and Tanya

# Contents

List of Appendices

# List of Figures

# List of Tables

नौसेना अध्यक्ष
CHIEF OF THE NAVAL STAFF

एडमिरल माधवेन्द्र सिंह
पी वी एस एम, ए वी एस एम, ए डी सी
**Admiral Madhvendra Singh**
PVSM, AVSM, ADC

रक्षा मंत्रालय
एकीकृत मुख्यालय (नौसेना)
नई दिल्ली - 110011
Integrated Headquarters
Ministry of Defence (Navy)
New Delhi - 110011

30 July 2004

# FOREWORD

The earth is essentially a water planet with the oceans and seas covering 71% of its surface. For long, nations have used the freedom of the seas to explore, conquer, pursue trade and increase their sphere of influence. There is now a growing realisation that the 21st century would be the century of the seas.

The increased focus on the oceans is due to the changing geo-strategic, geo-economic and technological scenarios in the maritime environment. This calls for a paradigm shift in the management perception of maritime affairs, as also new policy measures. This is especially relevant for India, since we are a maritime nation with over 90% of our trade by volume and 77% by value moving across the sea.

Recognising the importance of the seas to India and the need for safeguarding the nation's maritime interests, this book brings together the economic, environmental and security trinity that influences the formulation of maritime policy. It also highlights the need for synergy between the three for effective ocean governance.

The book covers a wide expanse and is written in a style that would appeal to those involved in the maritime affairs of the country, as well as the common man interested in the nation's maritime destiny. I would like to commend the author for his vision in bringing out, for the first time in the country, a comprehensive treatise on the management of maritime affairs.

(Madhvendra Singh)
Admiral
Chief of the Naval Staff

# Acknowledgement

The book is the successful culmination of a journey that commenced in July 2002 at the Centre for Research, United Services Institution of India (USI) under the aegis of the Admiral R.D. Katari chair for 2002-2003.

There are many people responsible to whom I owe my sincere gratitude. Many thanks to Lt. Gen. Satish Nambiar (Retd.) for the encouragement throughout the project period and Vice Admiral Premvir Das (Retd.) for his steadfast backing to the research work. My sincere thanks to Col. V.K. Singh (Retd.), for making my experience at the USI a memorable one.

My thanks to Col. P.K. Gautam (Retd.) and Vijendra Rana, for their support and the brainstorming sessions.

I am grateful to Dr. Rajat K. Baisya for helping me advance my thinking.

I owe a great deal to Admiral Madhvendra Singh, a visionary and great strategic thinker. His strategic thoughts in maritime affairs inspire me every day.

My thanks to all staff of the editors, reviewers and the publisher.

Finally, and most importantly my thanks to my parents, Chandra Mohan and Kumud for their support and my wife Neelam for her patience.

# Preface

The research has its genesis in the United Nations Convention on Law of the Sea in 1982, Agenda 21 and the Rio declaration in 1992, and the international security response in the maritime transportation sector after 11 September 2001, terrorist attacks on America.

In a democratic system, navies have functioned as an instrument of national policy. The relationship between navies and national policy is rapidly changing; it is becoming closely intertwined from the economic environmental and security perspective than ever before, making it even more complex in a dynamic marine environment.

The focus on Integrated Management provides a definite theme for maritime affairs. It is stressed throughout the research that Integrated Management of maritime affairs needs to be understood in the context of the principles of strategic management.

Knowledge and understanding of oceans is *fragmented* and *specialised*. An integrated management approach to maritime affairs is lacking in coherence. Such approaches are few in number too. As a result, a comprehensive approach rather than depth, has been chosen to familiarise the reader with the interdependent and indivisible nature of the multidisciplinary maritime sector.

The inspiration for this research has come from the educational experience at Southampton Institute, United Kingdom and the consequent application of learning at the Integrated Headquarters of the Ministry of Defence (Navy). The research aims to inspire others to an envisioned future of maritime India.

# 1

# The Ocean Future:

## Understanding the Maritime Dimension

In the 21st century, Oceans, the "common heritage of mankind" regarded as the 'last frontier' on earth, shall decisively influence world geo-politics, globalisation, socio-economic balance, and life of earth. The importance of the oceans has evolved, from a historical perspective, over the last 500 years. The world's oceans have afforded the human populace freedom, to explore, conquer and acquire natural resources, and wealth distributed over 29 per cent of the land. With 70.92 per cent of the earth's surface covered by water, the oceans encompass not only 2/3rd of the world surface but will impact the lives of 2/3rd of the world population by 2025.

History is indicative that in ancient times there was an understanding of the importance of maritime access for economic, political, and military purposes. In the beginning of the 15th century, at the fall of Rome, knowledge about the oceans was restricted to coastal trade (Coltrell, 1981). Around the year 1500, Portugal Sea Power changed the face of world geopolitics into the modern oceanic circle in which all states including land-locked states are now enmeshed (Kennedy, 1987 and Grove, 1990). Until then, the Ottoman Empire, India under the Moguls, China under the Ming dynasty, and the European State System were roughly at the same level of economic and technological development, and far superior to other scattered societies of Africa, Oceania, and America (Kennedy, 1987).

Amongst the complex motives of acquisitiveness, religious zeal, spirit of adventure, and discovery of new sea routes for trade, economic incentive was the principal motive for the Europeans to set out to discover sea routes and not the Asians (Edward d'Cruz, 1970, Parry, 1963, Prescott, 1985, Kennedy, 1976, Coltrell, 1981). The Europeans wanted to trade in Chinese silk and Indian Ivory, jewellery, pearls and precious stones, porcelain and precious woods, the finest muslins and calicoes, and the spices - pepper, cloves, nutmeg, cinnamon and ginger (Childe, 1969).

The quest for new sea routes was driven by the capture of Constantinople, in 1453, by the Ottoman Turks. Ever since, seaborne trade has remained the most significant single element of maritime access. With the fall of Constantinople, the Ottoman middlemen could control the main land lines of communication of East-West trade between Asia and Europe. The realisation that land can be politically controlled and walls could be created and zealously guarded to deny access, thus, led to the discovery of sea routes (Grove, 1990). The natural condition of the oceans in sharp contrast was "Freedom of the Seas" (Gray et al., 1989). The oceans have been the medium to control areas on land. The period from $15^{th}$ century until the Industrial Revolution in the $18^{th}$ Century, is known as the age of discovery, exploration, settlement or even reconnaissance - all implying the same thing (Prescott, 1985).

The rivalry amongst Europeans to achieve national power at sea coupled with the incentive of inflow of riches from overseas countries created a self generated interdependence between science and technology, industrial and economic strength, and military potential and foreign policy. Naval ship building, navigation and weaponry led to advances in science and technology driving industrial development. This became a significant index of economic strength, which in turn came to be reckoned as an index of military potential; not to forget its capacity to influence world geopolitics as an instrument of the nation's foreign policy. This virtuous circle of maritime activity shifted the centre of political gravity from land to oceans.

## Geography

The total water surface covers an area of 361,740,000 square kilometres ($Km^2$) compared with the total surface area of the earth of 509 million $Km^2$ (Couper, 1983). The oceans hold nearly 1.4 billion cubic kilometres ($Km^3$) of water and out of the 430, 000 $Km^3$ that evaporates from the oceans every year, 110,000 $Km^3$ falls as freshwater precipitation over land (WWF/IUCN Marine Policy). The ocean floor can be divided into continental margin and the deep ocean basin. The continental margin comprises of the continental shelf, slope and rise. Continental shelves are shallow platforms adjacent to the land masses. The seaward limit is usually defined by a shelf break, a distinct gradient change from the shelf to the steeper continental slope. The depth of water here ranges from 35m to 250m with the slope gradient ranging between 1:40 to 1:3. Seaward of the continental slope is the continental rise with gradients of 1:50 to 1:800. The deep ocean basin lies seaward of the continental margin.

Of the 192 member states in the United Nations (UN), 150 are coastal states and the remaining 42 are landlocked countries. (Appendix 1.) The Pacific Ocean with a coastline of 135,663 km is the largest ocean followed by the Atlantic Ocean with a coastline of 111,886 km, and the Indian

Ocean with a coastline of 66,526 km. The Indian Ocean is of utmost strategic importance in world affairs. Three of the six most important straits - Babel Mandeb, Dover, Dardanelles, Gibraltar, Hormuz and Malacca, on which the world's shipping concentrates, link the Indian Ocean to the other oceans. Babel Mandeb and Hormuz are major oil transit chokepoints with no alternative routes. The only viable alternative via Lombok to the Malacca adds nearly 1200nm to a voyage from the Persian Gulf to Japan.

The Indian Ocean extends only over one fifth of the world's total ocean surface. Its strategic waterways account for transportation of highest tonnage of goods globally - half the world's crude oil, container shipments and a third of the bulk cargo. The Indian Ocean area comprises 30 littoral states, five island states and 13 other island territories and 13 landlocked countries. According to the UN classification, countries which have access to the Indian Ocean only via a coastal state bordering the Indian Ocean and whose security is affected by development in those states form the Indian Ocean Region (Braun, 1983). By this definition, including the five Central Asian States of Kyrgyztan, Tajikistan, Uzbekistan, Kazakhstan and Turkmenistan amongst the landlocked states - whose maritime access lies either to the Baltic Sea or the Black Sea through the Caspian Sea or to the Indian Ocean, through Iran, Afghanistan and Pakistan - there are 53 countries and 13 other island territories in the Indian Ocean area (Appendix 2). The 53 countries represent over one third of the world's population; they account for two-thirds of the world's proven oil reserves, a third of its natural gas, 90 per cent of its diamonds, 60 per cent of its uranium and 40 per cent of its gold (Sinai, 2001). It is not surprising, therefore, for *Fernand Braudel* to have observed that the

Indian Ocean was a "*Weltwirtschaft*" or "World Economy" with India at the centre.

## Legal Perspective

The oceans have long been subject to the "Freedom of the Seas" doctrine. However, history of the law of the sea is a narration of the struggles for and against the doctrine of the freedom of the seas. As professor Verzijl states, "Historical research clearly proves, that freedom has no static content 'a priori', but is subject to continuous, at times even violent changes". Interestingly, it was not until the end of the Second World War in 1945 that the oceans began to witness a multitude of claims, counter claims and sovereignty disputes. By the late 60s, technological advances had led to a shift in the economic potential of oceans from the traditional use for navigation and fishing to exploitation of resources - from oil to tin, diamonds to gravel and metals to medicinal drugs.

The two principal sources of the law of the sea have been international customary law and treaties, and law of the sea emerges as one of the oldest components of international law (Brown, 1994). On 1 November 1967, Malta's Ambassador to the United Nations, Arvid Pardo, however, informed the United Nations General Assembly about the inadequacies of the current international law and the 'Freedom of the Seas' doctrine. It set in motion a process that spanned 15 years in an UN effort to overcome the plethora of claims by coastal states, preserve the freedom of navigation, conserve and optimally utilise the resources at sea, protect and preserve the marine environment and use the sea on a basis of 'equitable apportionment' so as to take into account the interests of mankind as a whole.

It was the third UN Convention on the Law of the Sea (UNCLOS-III) in 1982 that consolidated all past treaties, codified customary law and put in place new law for new issues. In one stroke, law of the sea evolved into hard law from soft law. UNCLOS III codified the oceans as the "Common Heritage of Mankind," to be managed responsibly and equitably for the benefit of all humanity. It was a global agreement. For the first time rights of land locked states in maritime affairs were also addressed. UNCLOS III has provided for the change in emphasis from 'Freedom of the Seas' to 'Control and Regulation'. It can be said that due to the ever increasing demands and abuses of the oceans, the international community was obliged to ensure the effective exercise of freedom by controlling and regulating it even more closely.

Coastal nations have been quick to exercise their rights by establishing their maritime zones for control and regulation. However, the effectiveness of control and regulation depends not only upon establishing jurisdiction in the coastal state legislation but actually exercising such jurisdiction in practice. Thus, there is a need to recognise the associated responsibilities if the rationale of UNCLOS III changing the emphasis from 'Freedom of the Seas' to 'Control and Regulation' is to be not only understood but also to be met. Similarly, there is a need to recognise that along with the 'Freedom of the Seas' there is a corresponding responsibility for those seeking to exercise that right. Forms of ocean governance have been rendered more complex by the increased number of coastal nation states and their differing interpretations of the UN Law of the Sea. With India as an example, Table 1.1 provides a glimpse of the differing interpretations of the Law of the Sea.

Table 1.1 Summary of India's Interpretation of the Law of the Sea

| Type | Date | Source | Limits | Interpretation and Responses |
|---|---|---|---|---|
| Territorial Sea | 1878 | U.K. Territorial Waters Act | 3nm | |
| | Mar 56 | Presidential Proclamation | 6nm | |
| | Sep 67 | Presidential Proclamation | 12nm | |
| | Aug 76 | Territorial Waters, Continental Shelf Exclusive Economic Zone & Other Maritime Zones Act, No. 80 | 12nm | Foreign warships must provide notice prior to entering territorial sea. This requirement is not recognised by the US. The US protested requirement in 1976 and 1983 and conducted operational assertions in 1985-89, 1991-1994, 1996, 1997 and 1999. |

| Type | Date | Source | Limits | Interpretation and Responses |
|---|---|---|---|---|
| **Archipelagic, Straight Baselines, & Historic Claims** | Jan 77 | Notice/Act No. 80 & Law No. 41 (1 Jun 79) | | Waters of Palk Bay between coast and boundary with Sri Lanka claimed as internal waters; waters of Gulf of Mannar between coast and maritime boundary claimed as historic waters. This claim is not recognised by the US. The US conducted opertional assertions in 1993 and 1994 and Operational challenge to the Gulf of Mannar claim in 1999. |
| **Contiguous Zone** | Dec 56 | Presidential Proclamation | 12nm | |
| | Jan 77 | Notice/Act No. 80 | 24nm | Claimed powers in contiguous zone include taking of measures necessary with respect to security. This claim is not recognised by the US. |

| Type | Date | Source | Limits | Interpretation and Responses |
|---|---|---|---|---|
| **Continental Shelf** | Aug 55 | Presidential Proclamation | | |
| | Aug 76 | Act No. 80 | 200/CM | |
| **Fishing zone/ Exclusive Economic Zone (EEZ)** | Nov 56 | Presidential Proclamation | | Reserved right to declare fishery conservation zone up to 100nm from outer limit of territorial sea. |
| | Dec 56 | Presidential Proclamation | 6nm | Fishing zone. |
| **Fishing zone/ Exclusive Economic Zone (EEZ)** | Aug 76 | Act No. 80 | 200nm | Enabling legislation for EEZ: claimed exclusive jurisdiction over construction/operation of artificial islands/structures/"devices" and over scientific research; recognised freedom of navigation/ over flight "subject to the exercise by India to its rights within the zone." |

| Type | Date | Source | Limits | Interpretation and Responses |
|---|---|---|---|---|
| | | | | The US and UK does not recognise requirement of prior notification for scientific research (military survey) in the EEZ by warships and undertook research in 2001. |
| | Jan 98 | Naval HQ<br>Navarea Notice | | Requires prior notification (24 hours) from all vessels entering EEZ with hazardous cargoes including dangerous goods and chemicals, oil, noxious liquid and harmful substances and radioactive material. This requirement is not recognised by the US and was protested in 1998. The US conducted an operational assertion in 1999. |

| Type | Date | Source | Limits | Interpretation and Responses |
|---|---|---|---|---|
| LOS Convention | Dec 82 | | | Signed. |
| | Jul 94 | | | Signed Part XI Agreement subject to ratification. |
| | Jun 95 | | | Ratified Convention and Part XI Agreement, with declaration claiming the right to require prior consent for other States to carry out military exercises and manoeuvres in its EEZ or on its continental shelf. This claim is not recognised by the US. The US protested the claim in 1998 and conducted an operational assertion in 1999. |

*Source: US/UK Operational Assertions:*

1. Department of Defence Issuance 2005. Washington Headquarters Services http://www.dtic.mil/whs/directives/corres/20051m_040201/indiafinal.doc.
2. *Times of India*, 01 February 2001: US, UK ships caught snooping in Indian waters.

Through the 1990's the legal and institutional support for ocean governance has continued to be strengthened through a number of conventions, agreements and programmes of action that were negotiated, adopted or entered into force to address different issues. As many as 40 international agreements and programmes have been negotiated, adopted or entered into force in an effort to promote peace and security, as well as, sustainable development of the oceans. The range of international agreements dealing with all aspects of maritime affairs have contributed to international norm-setting for ocean governance, but implementation at the national level continues to be a challenge. National authorities need to act now in addressing the challenge of implementation.

## Changing Maritime Environment

Under the vast international setting the case for management of maritime affairs is easy to make. However, the management change is hard to lead. The change requires a shift in mindset and comes from external pressure and enlightened leadership. Nations need to adapt to the changing maritime environment and therefore face the need to change.

The change in the maritime environment began to evolve in the early 20$^{th}$ century, with discovery of offshore oil and a growing realisation of the potential to exploit ocean resources, such as minerals and fish. The speed of change accelerated over the past three decades due to a perceptible shift in mindset from one of "apparent abundance" to "growing scarcity" of ocean resources, and due to the increasing ocean uses, from "accommodation" to "conflict". These changes in the basic condition of ocean use, raised questions on the legal status of oceans from one of "Freedom of the Seas" to that of "Control and Regulation". A variety of factors have contributed to these changes in the nature of the maritime environment.

From a security perspective, the end of the cold war has witnessed the emergence of new categories of maritime security challenges - environmental degradation, resource scarcity, transnational crime, piracy, drug trafficking, illegal immigration, terrorism and so on. It also eroded the bipolar model of international relations bringing an increased opportunity to address global problems with a growing acceptance of a wider conception of peace and security. Many of the issues are beyond the capacity of individual states to tackle alone, even though tough, independent measures can be taken to reduce their vulnerability to certain threats. From 1984 to June 2002, 2,678 incidents of piracy and armed attacks were reported to the International Maritime Organization (IMO). 276 incidents of migrant smuggling, involving 12,426 migrants, were reported to IMO from the end of 2000 to 30 April 2002 (UNDOALOS, 2002). The empowerment of transnational non-state actors necessitates international cooperation to deny them access to sanctuaries, weaponry, finances and other resources. Consequently, despite the growth in sea denial capability of a number of nations, there is increasing interdependence among these nations for maritime security.

From an economic perspective, the breaking down of economic boundaries, globalisation and aid for eliminating poverty has had a significant impact on governance and security. Trade, aid, and security are mutually supportive in theory. Trade leading to growth in economic and social exchange between groups, combined with international standards of governance to preserve peace, and balanced by transfer of payments should lead to more harmonious and equitable societies. The reality is that globalisation of weakly governed markets coupled with misuse of international development assistance and aggressive promotion of unbalanced trade is straining traditional international and national mechanisms for preserving peace. (Halle, *et.al.* 2002)

From a social perspective, there is growing dependency on ocean use for resource and transit of goods by all nations leading to unplanned development and decline of traditional sectors. Uncontrolled development in the port and tourism or other sectors destroys cultural heritage and dilutes the social fabric of the coastal population. The carrying capacity of the coastal zone is exceeded thereby polluting and degrading natural resources, destroying the landscapes and reducing the quality of life of the coastal populace. The consumption of uncooked sewage-contaminated shellfish causes some 2.5 million cases of infectious hepatitis each year, at a cost of approximately $10 billion annually (UNDOALOS, 2002). In addition to this, the decline of traditional sectors like inland fisheries, struggling to remain competitive, is leading to unemployment, emigration and social instability. The capacity to accommodate has steadily eroded and conflicts among competing uses have become ubiquitous.

From a technological perspective, accelerated growth in science and technology has led to the discovery of new uses and the potential to exploit them. For instance, new advances in technology have allowed mankind to go further offshore and deeper into the oceans. Life on the seabed, which was once thought of as existing only in the shallow waters of the continental shelf, has now been found at depths of more than 4,000 feet. The accelerated growth in science and technology has also led to the better understanding of oceans for taking immediate action to prevent global warming and sea-level rise which threatens the survival of some countries, like Small Island Developing States (SIDS) and low-lying coastal States. The global average sea level has risen by 10 to 25 centimetres over the past 100 years. Models project that sea levels will rise another 15 to 95 cm by 2100 - with the "best estimate" at 50 cm (UNDOALOS, 2002). At the same time advances in science and technology has also added to the vulnerability of the oceans. For instance, increasing trade is making demands for a more efficient cargo transport. The development of faster and larger ships with zero tolerance for the negative environment impacts such as emissions, discharges of bilge water and tank washings, and introduction of harmful alien species into new environments through ship ballast water is placing enormous pressure on the marine environment.

From a legal perspective, the new UN 'Law of the Sea' (1982) has not only increased the demand for uses of the oceans but promises to alter radically the traditional freedom of access enjoyed by maritime powers in the past. Now, more than one-third of the world's oceans fall within the Exclusive Economic Zone (EEZ) of coastal states. The 200 nm EEZ is no longer regarded as the "High Seas" and gives coastal states exclusive rights with respect to natural resources and other economic activities and the right to exercise jurisdiction over marine scientific research and environmental protection. The economic significance of EEZs is evident from the fact that 90 per cent of the world fish stocks are now within national jurisdictions. Further, the High Seas, representing another two-third's of the earth's surface are beyond national jurisdiction and the International Seabed Authority has come to be vested with the control of its seabed and resources.

From an environmental perspective, the balance between human life and the environment which assumed international dimensions since the 1970's has come to be recognised as one of the pillars of sustainable development. Growth in the intensity of ocean use is impinging on the carrying capacity and levels of sustainable use of the marine environment. It is estimated that approximately 27 per cent of coral reefs are at high risk of degradation due to direct human impact and the effects of climate change. It is predicted that a further 50 to 60 per cent of the world's reefs may be destroyed within the next 30 years unless urgent measures are taken (UNDOALOS, 2002). Oceans are no longer considered to exist in isolation from land. Land-based sources are responsible for 80 per cent of the pollution of the oceans while dumping of wastes and other matter accounts for 10 per cent of pollutants in the oceans affecting the most productive areas of the marine environment. Ocean pollution is estimated to cause some 250 million cases of gastroenteritis and upper respiratory disease every year, costing societies worldwide about $1.6 billion a year (UNDOALOS, 2002).

From a political perspective, effective forms of ocean governance have been rendered more complex by the increased number of nation states and their differing interpretations of the UN Law of the Sea. The major maritime powers benefit from the current arrangements or from the absence of them. This is even more so when traditional negotiating blocks - like for disarmament, development, trade and investment - are much less in evidence in the case of the oceans. Further, the economic ideology of nations is placing heavy reliance on the market and role of private enterprise and therefore nations are not receptive to regulatory mechanisms for the oceans.

The absence of regulatory mechanisms has led to the abuse of oceans. Growing awareness of the problems of the oceans has not yet permeated to individual behaviour. Nations left to their own devices are unable to dispense answers to questions relating to peace, security, equity and the environment. As a consequence, the management of maritime affairs is flawed - imposed by the complexity of the issue and the realisation that our "knowledge" to effectively take into account the multidisciplinary and interdependent issues is still inadequate.

## Valuing the maritime resource base

The economic value of the oceans defies easy measurement. Oceans cover almost three-quarters of the Earth's surface, comprise nine-tenths of its water resources and are home to over 97 per cent of all life. The oceans provide a natural route for communication, transportation and trade, what with approximately 90 per cent of international trade being transported by sea. The world's merchant fleet exceeds 85,000 ships and the value of seaborne trade and shipping is $ 155 billion annually. The oceans are a major source of food and employment. About 90 per cent of the world's fisheries fall under the jurisdiction of coastal states. Every year, almost 90 million tons of fish are captured globally, providing by far the largest source of wild protein for human consumption. The world fishery production projection for 2010, according to the Food and Agricultural Organisation (FAO), ranges between 107 and 144 million tons. In the primary capture fisheries and aquaculture production alone, the fishing industry provides work to some 36 million people each year. Marine minerals have been estimated to generate nearly US $ one trillion every year. These valuable minerals include offshore oil and gas, gold, tin, diamonds, sand and gravel, which can be found both within and beyond the limits of national jurisdiction. Offshore oil production accounts for about 30 per cent of total world oil production, and offshore gas production accounts for about half of world production. Offshore oil production worldwide grew from about 13,500 million barrels per day in the early 1980s to about 18,600 million barrels per day in the mid-1990s, an increase of 37 percent. In the same period, offshore gas production worldwide grew from about 28,300 to 35,900 million cubic feet per day, an increase of 27 per cent. Huge deposits of frozen compounds of methane gas (methane hydrates) can be found at 600 to 1,500 feet below the ocean floor on continental margins throughout the world. These ocean-floor deposits are a potentially enormous source of energy. Scientists estimate that they contain twice the amount of organic carbon as all recoverable and non-recoverable oil, gas and coal deposits on Earth. More than half of the world's population lives near the sea, at a density twice the global average. By 2025, nearly two thirds of the world's population will live within 60 kilometres of the coast. The combined value of ocean resources and uses is estimated to be about US $7 trillion per year (UNDOALOS, 2002). Historically, the oceans have been fished and navigated for millennia and have been a major focus for the development of human society (Volger, 1995). The 21st century is indeed the "century of the seas."

## Strategic Use

The principal reason for Hugo Grotius' "*Mare liberum*" or the concept of "Freedom of the Seas" was to remove and prevent restrictions on international trade (IWCO, 1998). Ever since major maritime powers for their security interests have restated the concept to imply as much 'free and open' military use of the oceans as possible. Military activities in the air, surface and sub surface ocean space has never been legally challenged and rests on the core concepts of *'res communis*' and 'freedom of navigation'.

The strategic value of naval forces is their enormous capacity for geographical flexibility and of increasing or reducing in a relative short time the scale of military pressure in distant regions (Couper, 1983). Navies thus form a crucial politico-strategic factor that in conjunction with other factors - economic, social and cultural - lays the basis for staking a claim to world leadership (Modelski and Thompson, 1988). Every global war has been a contest for world leadership and has been decisively fought across the oceans (Modelski and Thompson, 1988). Ironically, over the course of history many countries have maintained large armies, but those that have built and provided for large navies are only ten or even fewer (Gray *et al.*, 1989). Interestingly, global wars have taken place at the end and beginning of each century.

The leadership in global politics coupled with a strong national navy constitutes 'Sea Power' (Modelski and Thompson, 1988). Conceptualisation of what constitutes sea power began long before Mahan in 1890, but it was he who first articulated it (Hill, 1986). Like Mahan, Corbett, Castex, Custance, Colomb, Richmond and other writers were all interested in war and dominance. Historians like Mackinder, Pannicker and Fisher fundamentally agree that early 15$^{th}$ century transformed the political equation and economic balance in world affairs heralding four centuries of authority based on control of the seas (Kennedy, 1976).

The modes of usage and control of the sea appropriate to that usage defined as a nation's "Maritime Power", goes beyond the Mahanian paradigm of sea power (Modelski and Thompson, 1988). It has often been argued - of late - by Admiral Gorshkov that a nation's sea power is determined not only by the weapons and armed forces with which it can affect events at sea but also by its mercantile marine, fishing and oceanographic fleets and its maritime outlook and tradition (Alford, 1980). In the 21st century, "Maritime Power" may be defined as the *'maritime resource of a nation's power'*. The world's oceans being one interconnected system, the "*maritime resource of a nation's power*", that is the political outlook, level of international and regional cooperation, naval power, coastal communities, mercantile marine, port infrastructure, living and non-living resources, ship design, building, repair and maintenance, coastal shipping and inland waterways, oceanographic science and technology, marine biodiversity and a legal regime for oceans to influence world geo-politics and economic trade, would arguably constitute the nation's maritime power.

Sea Power or "Command of the Sea" as conceived by Mahan, however, lost its validity in early 20th century due to the sheer pace of technological change (Gray et al., 1989). As a result, modern interpretation of "Command of the Sea" has been that of "Sea Control" - a control usually limited both in time and space. The limited concept of "Sea Denial" is however more prevalent. The new 'Law of the Sea' has witnessed a growth in "Sea Denial" capability, as nations in the use and control of the sea need the means to assert their rights and carry out their duties in the newly defined 200nm EEZ. Such concepts, although strategically defensive in nature, at the tactical level frequently involve conduct of offensive operations by navies alone in their attainment for the projection of power by a nation for fulfilling its national interests. "Sea Control" and

"Sea Denial" cannot be construed as "Sea Power" which deals with the interconnectedness of force, economy and geography as originally thought of by Mahan.

What then constitutes a nation's "Sea Power"? 'Freedom of the Seas' across 71 per cent of the world's surface left the human populace fiercely competing for the remaining 29 per cent of the land. As a result, land which has always been in control and the sea which has always been used to control other areas on land, saw the emergence of new nation states and advances in technology (Grove, 1990). With booming population and shrinking land availability, five centuries down the line, the 21st century has come to be spoken of as the "century of the seas" as the seas with their seemingly inexhaustible resources have increasingly to meet human needs of food and living. Ironically, the focus on the seas is not for creating nation states but for safeguarding use of the sea of existing nation states - within the 200nm Exclusive Economic Zone - in close proximity of their coastlines. Hence, in defining "Maritime Power" the linking of the political, strategic, diplomatic, economic, social, cultural, environmental, legal and technological factors helps to lay the foundation of a nation's "Sea Power" in the 21st century as the *"power to govern the sea."* There are four attributes of Sea Power - power to govern the sea:

a) Ruling with authority and constitutionally conducting the maritime policy, actions and affairs of the nation.

b) Being in military command of the sea and regulating proceedings at sea as required by national interests.

c) Constituting a law, rule, standard or principle for the nation at sea.

d) Acting or functioning at sea in a manner of governing or control.

## Ocean Governance - A Challenge

Mahan a reticent, un-likable naval captain of middling reputation (Gattuso *et.al.*, 2001) who captured the nation's imagination, has the greatest relevance today in his political vision, his sense of destiny and his efforts to persuade his own government that its future greatness lay in the further exploration of its maritime potential (Coltrell, 1981). For the future, a nation's power to govern the sea and develop its maritime resource for long term economic prosperity holds the key to sustaining economic growth, ensuring protective security and positioning itself as a leader in world geopolitics. It is now established that in the oceans, economic development, environmental protection, and maritime security are interdependent and indivisible. The trinity of ocean policy spheres derive their growing integration from the regimen of the Exclusive Economic Zone (EEZ) defined under the UN Law of the Sea, and are the cornerstones of 'Ocean Governance' for the 21st century. Broadly, the use of the sea for national interests involves passage of trade and exploitation of ocean resources, protecting the marine ecosystem from environmental damage, and safeguarding the sovereign and territorial integrity of the nation.

Although law of the sea has evolved over five centuries, the present body of rules, agreements, treaties, law and institutions have developed in the last five decades, in a global attempt to provide a system of ocean governance. The difficulty lies in incorporating the ocean dimension into a number of pre-existing sectoral structures, such as, fisheries under the Food and Agriculture Organisation (FAO). The result has been a proliferation of treaties with independent action plans, strategies and funding mechanisms. The expansion of legal instruments makes it increasingly difficult for a nation to translate these instruments into a verifiable expression of national preferences.

While legal entities and national boundaries may be important for ease of management; the management of maritime affairs is not legal or political but operational embracing the entire process to focus on performance across the complete range of maritime activities. Performance therefore will increasingly have to be based on balancing short term gains with long term prosperity. The normal emphasis on returns on investment as a means of performance will have to undergo change. Performance will now have to be defined non-financially in terms of the knowledge within the organisation and the sharing of knowledge amongst stakeholders. To address the overlapping spheres of management of maritime affairs in a period of political, social, economic, technological, environmental, legal and security transformation requires acceptance of these new fundamentals of "knowledge within" and "sharing of knowledge" in determining what constitutes performance within the organisation.

Over the past few decades there has been recognition of the need to create an appropriate institutional framework, but the recognition has so far failed to result in a coherent system of ocean governance. The information shared and polices adopted by established administrative institutions at the international level remains fragmented among the sectoral agencies at all levels of governance - international, national, state and local. As a consequence, the national framework worldwide parallels the sectoral international structure like fisheries under the Ministry of Agriculture in India. Line ministries and departments responsible for individual sectors such as fisheries and aquaculture, ports and shipping, oil and gas, tourism, environment and maritime security rarely coordinate their work due to the lack of a clear picture of national objectives and commitments. The challenge to developing a nation's maritime resource and its power to govern the sea is adopting an integrated management approach to ocean governance.

With a multitude of maritime activities - fisheries, oil and gas, shipping, ports, mineral exploration, tourism, biodiversity - competing for the same ocean space, what is needed is an "organisation that fits the task" for ocean governance in the sustainable development of oceans. Generally, nations first define a mission that defines strategy and strategy defines structure which leads to conflict of interests between the resultant sectoral ministries and departments. In effect, a sectoral mission leads to sectoral strategy which in turn leads to a sectoral structure. It creates a work culture in which strategy formulation, implementation and control is rarely coordinated. On the other hand, an integrated management approach to ocean governance becomes the "specific and distinguishing organ of all organisations" engaged in maritime affairs. It therefore must have the endorsement of all the stakeholders for achieving policy coordination, policy consistency and policy coherence.

## The Oceanic circle

The Indian Ocean which extends only over one fifth of the world's total ocean surface is the one that is of utmost strategic importance in world affairs for the 21$^{st}$ century.

Under the UN Law of the Sea more than one-third of the world's oceans fall within the Exclusive Economic Zone (EEZ) of coastal nations. The economic value of the oceans defies easy measurement. In the 21st century, *Maritime Power* may be defined as the *"maritime resource of a nation's power"* and Sea Power may be defined as the *"power to govern the sea."*

It is now established that in the oceans, economic development, environmental protection, and maritime security are interdependent and indivisible. The challenge to developing a nation's maritime resource and its power to govern the sea lies in adopting an integrated management approach to ocean governance.

# 2

# Integrated Management:
## In Search of Sustainable Development

To achieve sustainability in the new millennium, the first step is to bring all users and uses of the maritime (ocean and coastal) zone under some type of management (Freidheim, 1999). Maritime means a conglomerate of anything connected with the sea, pertaining to the sea, bordering on the sea and living near or in the sea. The management of the maritime zone is therefore multidisciplinary in nature, balancing economic activity, social equity and environmental quality (ECDP, 1999) for sustainable development; and security is an essential precondition to Sustainable Development. Without security, social institutions cannot function, people cannot plan for the future and financiers cannot make investments (Halle, *et.al.*, 2002).

Among the pressures on the maritime zone is the growing dependence on the oceans for the transit of raw materials which together with globalisation of weakly governed markets impinges on the sustainable development of oceans. The new Law of the Sea has witnessed unprecedented ocean development in the past two decades. Expanding economic activities in the Exclusive Economic Zone (EEZ) such as offshore energy, port development, renewable energy, coastal tourism, marine leisure, aquaculture, transportation, communication, and fishing has resulted not only in pressures of social instability but even security considerations. Social instability has been a consequence of growing coastal population and loss of traditional employment not to forget the environmental concerns of increased pollution and habitat degradation. These pressures make the maritime zone a dynamic and complex area for management (Olsen *et.al.*, 1997).

Given the importance of ocean resources, in today's complex economy the management of maritime affairs is of strategic importance to all nations. The increased demand for uses of the oceans has radically altered the traditional freedom of access enjoyed by maritime powers as we witness a growth in sea denial capability. Concurrently, concerns of over exploitation has called for Integrated Management (IM) and Sustainable Development (SD) of the maritime zone. In emphasising that the problems of the ocean space are closely interrelated and need to be considered as a whole, UNCLOS III laid the foundation of a framework for management of maritime affairs. The guidelines, principles, objectives and actions needed for the management of maritime affairs were developed over time by the Brutland Report (1987) "Our Common Future", prepared by the World Commission on Environment and Development (WECD), "Agenda 21 and the Rio declaration (1992)" of the United Nations Commission on Environment and Development (UNCED) and report of the Independent World Commission on the Oceans (1998) titled "The Ocean: Our Future". All emphasise the fundamental importance of ocean governance for maintaining peace and security, and sustainable development of the oceans, which is also the corner stone of UNCLOS III. Principle 25 of the Rio Declaration upholds that peace and security, development, and environmental protection are interdependent and indivisible. The change in emphasis from "Freedom of the Seas" to "Control and Regulation" in the management of maritime affairs has become even more evident after 11 September 2001 terrorist attacks on America. The threat of maritime terrorism has brought swift and unprecedented legislation by the international community for security of shipping and ports. The timeline of events that lays emphasis on ocean governance for sustainable development of oceans is shown in Table 2.1.

**Table 2.1: Timeline for Sustainable Development**

| Year | Event |
|---|---|
| 1945 | On 28 September 1945 President Truman of the United States, makes twin declarations relating to fisheries and continental shelf extending the coastal jurisdiction to 200nm in areas of the high seas contiguous to the coasts of the United States. |
| 1958 | The First United Nations Conference on the Law of the Sea is convened. |
| 1960 | The Second United Nations Conference on the Law of the Sea is convened. |
| 1967 | Arvid Pardo, President of Malta, coins the phrase 'Common Heritage of Mankind' in highlighting the inadequacies of the current international law on the oceans. |
| 1968 | The Committee on the Peaceful Uses of the Seabed and the Ocean Floor beyond the Limits of National Jurisdiction is established. |
| 1972 | UN Stockholm conference on the human environment represents the first effort by the international community to deal with |

| Year | Event |
|---|---|
| | environmental problems on a comprehensive basis by creating the United Nations Environmental Programme (UNEP). |
| 1973 | The Third United Nations Conference on the Law of the Sea opens. |
| 1982 | Convention on the Law of the Sea is adopted by the Third United Nations Conference. |
| 1987 | World Commission on Environment and Development (WCED) in its report 'Our Common Future' states: "looking into the next century, the commission is convinced that Sustainable Development if not survival itself depends upon significant advances in the management of the oceans." |
| 1988 | Convention for the Suppression of Unlawful Acts Against Safety of Maritime Navigation and the Protocol on the Safety of Fixed platforms located on the continental shelf (SUA, 1988). |
| 1991 | Organisation for Economic Cooperation and Development Guidelines. |
| 1992 | Earth Summit. UN Conference on Environment and Development (UNCED) at Rio. Agreements reached on Agenda 21 underlying Integrated Management and Sustainable Development. |
| 1993 | Commission on Sustainable Development established to oversee implementation of Agenda 21. |
| 1993 | World Bank Guidelines. |

| Year | Event |
|---|---|
| 1993 | International Union for Conservation of Natural Resources (IUCN) Guidelines. |
| 1994 | The Convention on Law of the Sea enters into force. |
| 1994 | World Coast Conference report. |
| 1995 | The International Seabed Authority becomes operational. |
| 1995 | United Nations Environmental Programme Guidelines. |
| 1996 | The International Tribunal for the Law of the Sea becomes operational. |
| 1997 | The Commission on the Limits of the Continental Shelf holds its first session. |
| 1998 | International Year of the Oceans. |
| 2001 | Review of SUA 1988 to address maritime terrorism. |
| 2002 | World Summit on Sustainable Development. |
| 2002 | IMO adopts the International Ship and Port Facility Security(ISPS) Code. |
| 2004 | ISPS Code comes into force on 01 July 2004. |

## The Maritime Zone

The maritime zone may be looked at as (Dronkers and de Vries, 1999):

a) A neighbourhood with a unique socio-cultural entity that offers fresh air, natural light, and long range views of landscapes and seascapes that provide a distinct culture and way of life over centuries. About two-thirds of the world's population is projected to live within the coastal region by 2025 (Chapter 17 Agenda 21 in Olsen etal., 1997). Consequently, two-thirds of world's largest cities are going to be situated on coasts (Cicin-Sain and Knecht, 1998).

b) A geographic area where the land and sea interact through the dynamics of natural processes. The boundary of this maritime zone encloses a space, which extends from the sea across the land-sea interface to an inland limit. It is difficult to define such an all-embracing area in terms of physical or administrative boundaries. Figure 2.1 illustrates the possible limits to define the geographic extent of the maritime zone. Ideally, the inland limit must encompass all activities that have a direct impact on the maritime zone. The concept of EEZ has transformed the status of the coastal waters out to the 200 nautical mile limit. Thus, ideally, the seaward limit must extend up to 200 nautical miles.

c) A region of simultaneous and continually increasing land and sea based economic activity. "A few boxes of undersized herring cannot stand in the way of 500 000 containers" (*Saiz*, 1989). With each activity competing for the same space the quote reflects a typical conflict of interests between different economic user groups. The region of land and sea based economic use can be classified into a number of basic categories that reflect the fundamental human activities involved (Figure 2.2).

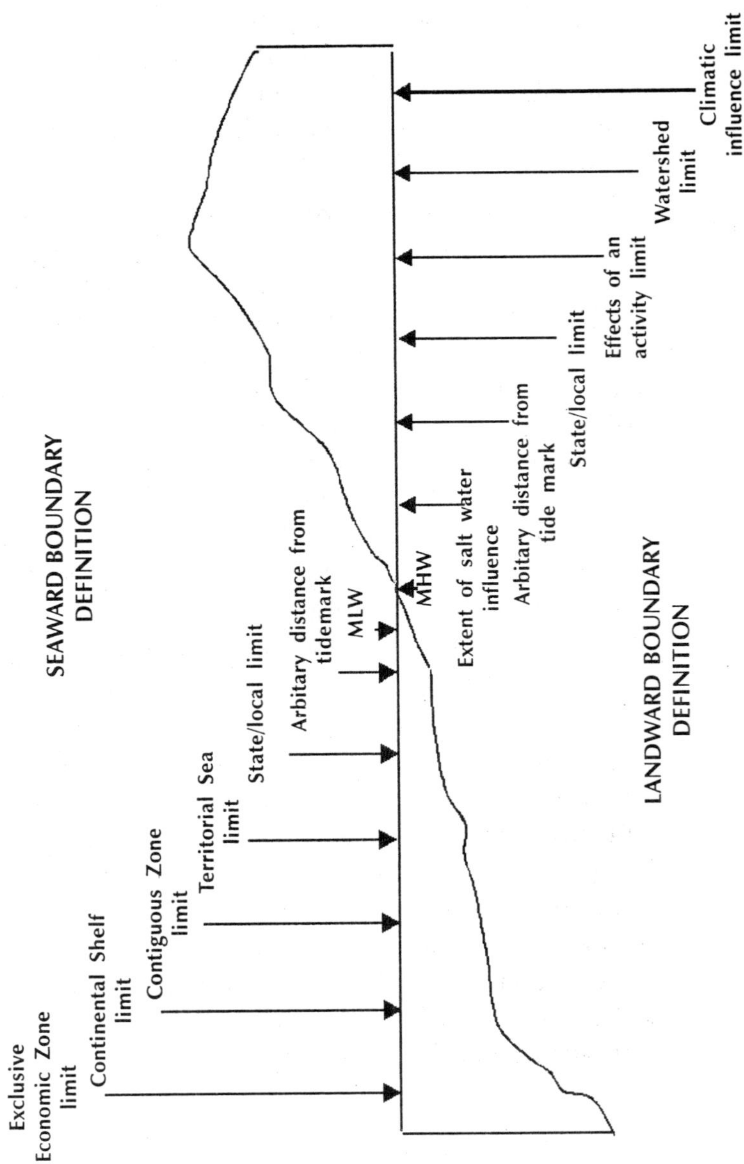


Figure 2.1 Possible Boundary Limits for IM

Figure 2.2: Range of Activities in the Maritime Zone

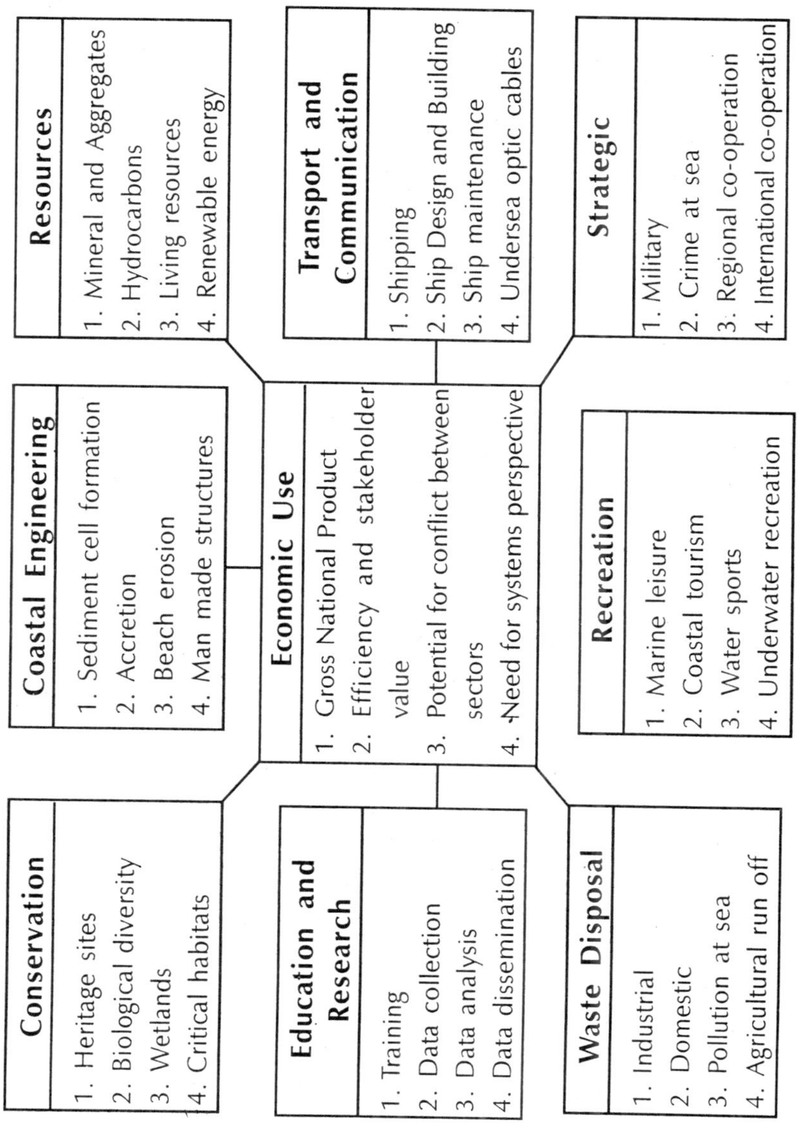

The dynamics of natural processes manifested by continually increasing economic activity across difficult-to-define boundaries, due to the unique socio-cultural entity, makes the maritime zone a highly complex system for management. Certain problems have been identified (ECDP, 1999):

a) Legislation and policy have been sectorally based and uncoordinated.

b) Inappropriate and isolated sectoral planning decisions have often worked against long term interests.

c) Rigid bureaucratic systems have limited local creativity and adaptability.

d) Local initiatives have lacked adequate resources and support from higher administrative levels.

e) Management has lacked vision and has been based on a very limited understanding of the coastal processes.

f) Scientific research and data have been isolated from end-users.

There appears to be growing consensus on the outlines of a general model for management of maritime affairs. The writings of Kay and Alder (1999), Cicin-Sain and Knecht (1998), Clark (1998), Kenchington (1993), Lowry (1993), Miles (1996), Olsen (1999), Smith (2000), Sorensen (1997) and Thia-Eng (1997) stress the dynamic nature of the maritime zone with an emphasis on integration. The EC Demonstration Programme can be said to have summarised their writings to define Integrated Management (IM) as a dynamic, continuous and iterative process designed to promote sustainable development of the maritime zone. Based on all this IM can be said to take into account:

a) *Spatial integration* or the need to consider the challenges of the ocean space as a whole.

b) *Temporal integration* or the linking of long term vision to medium term targets to short term action.

c) *Stakeholder integration* or the promoting of genuine partnerships between government, industry, community, scientific institutions and other stakeholders so that there is a cooperative approach to problem solving as the problems are too complex to be resolved by any one group acting alone.

d) *Sectoral integration* or the development of horizontal linkages across sectors so that there is a coordinated approach to economic development.

e) *Institutional integration* or the establishment of vertical linkages between institutional levels so that there is a collaborative approach to local, state, national and international policy development efforts, and governance.

Undoubtedly, national prosperity requires sustained economic growth and resource development to increase productivity and national income. However, alongside economic growth, the social - intersociety and intergenerational equity; environmental - resource conservation and protection; and security - sovereignty considerations and good order at sea, issues also require attention for sustainable development. These issues when not addressed accumulate over time and have consequences that do not show up in the shorter time-horizon typical of economic policy making (Five-year plans in India). Unless the transformation of society, protection of the environment and security of national assets are addressed integrally with economic development, growth itself will be jeopardised over the long term. Thus, sustainable development over the long term is not only based on the inherent principle of economic well being, social justice, and environmental quality, but peace and security are principally essential to achieving sustainable development and ensuring that it actually benefits all. Drawing from the body of literature over the past three decades, one can summarise the vision, goals, principles and initiatives of Integrated Management of maritime affairs for Sustainable Development (Table 2.2).

**Table 2.2: Scope of Integrated Management**

| Scope | Core Values |
|---|---|
| **Vision** | Politically correct, Economically efficient, environmentally sustainable, socially equitable, culturally sensitive and technologically sound governance for sustainable maritime development. |
| **Goals** | * **Politically correct** development to safeguard maritime interests and strengthen national security.<br>* **Economically efficient** development to improve quality of life and employment opportunities.<br>* **Environmentally sustainable** development to preserve the quality of the marine environment.<br>* **Socially equitable** development to provide inter-society and inter-generational equity.<br>* **Culturally sensitive** development to protect the culture of coastal communities. |

| Scope | Core Values |
|---|---|
| **Principles** | * **Technologically sound**- development to advance the understanding and usage of the ocean space.<br><br>* **Careful decision making**- As far as possible make decisions that are based on the best available information and knowledge.<br><br>* **Precautionary principle**-Use comprehensive methods of political, economic, environmental, social, cultural and technological assessment in deciding upon measures for Sustainable Development of the maritime zone.<br><br>* **User pays principle**- User must pay part costs of measures to prevent, control and reduce damage to the biological diversity, seascapes and coastal landscapes.<br><br>* **Public participation**- Develop private-public partnerships to gather valuable insights on management needs and economic opportunities and secure support of the user for fully accomplishing the goals.<br><br>* **Public access to information**- Make available accurate, timely and documented official information on proposed development activities for two-way communications among government agencies, user groups and local communities.<br><br>* **Best available technology**- Use of water saving technologies and non contaminant material for maritime infrastructure require |

| Scope | Core Values |
|---|---|
| | access to transfer of technology for attainment of Sustainable Development of the maritime zone.<br><br>* **Best environmental practice**- To control the scale of activities in relation to the natural, cultural and physical characteristics of the surrounding area undertake Strategic Impact Assessment (SIA) for considering the cumulative influences of the development.<br><br>* **Ecological Integrity**- Afford strict conservation status to outstanding natural features and important flora and fauna habitats. |
| **Initiatives** | * **Take a long-term view**- The dynamic and complex environment necessitates continuous updating and amendments to the distinct elements of a coherent and overarching strategy for sustainable maritime development.<br><br>* **Adopting adaptive management**- Adopt an incremental cyclic process based on principles of participatory democracy and reliable knowledge that applies the best available science to the issues that a management initiative is working to address.<br><br>* **An integrated approach**- Horizontally and vertically integrated planning and management are necessary by practitioners to effectively and efficiently plan and manage the maritime zone for Sustainable Development. |

| Scope | Core Values |
|---|---|
| | * **Collaborative culture**- Effective participation of all the stakeholders is necessary to achieve commitment, ownership and shared responsibility in accomplishing the goals.<br><br>* **Multidisciplinary training**- Develop human capacity in multidisciplinary understanding of the activities in the maritime zone to demonstrate that effective resource management is possible and sustainable.<br><br>* **Best practice guidelines**- Highlight best practice guidelines to encourage change in the mindsets of all the stakeholders<br><br>* **Measure goals**- develop indicators to measure the extent to which any action is sustainable and consequently the effect of any change in that action so as to objectively tell the progress towards sustainable maritime development.<br><br>* **Conflict resolution mechanisms**- Initiate public policy making in which all stakeholders can negotiate for effective conflict resolution.<br><br>* **Interdisciplinary research**- Evaluate the maritime zone in its entirety through interdisciplinary research for cross sectoral planning and management. |

Using Porter's five Ps of strategy - Plan, Ploy, Pattern, Position, Perspective - (Mintzberg, 1998), an attempt has been made in relating IM to principles of strategy (Table 2.3). It can be argued that IM is a question of strategic management that broadly encompasses the areas of strategy formulation, implementation and control (Miller, 1998). In essence, IM integrates various functions, is oriented towards organisation wide goals, considers a broad range of stakeholders, entails multiple time horizons and is concerned with both efficiency and effectiveness.

Essentially, IM emphasises integration across scales of time and space, active participation of stakeholders and an incremental iterative approach to problem solving. Of the 150 coastal states, except for Taiwan all are participating in one or more international IM efforts (Sorenson, 2000). In 2001, there were 98 nations engaged in developing an IM strategy. In terms of institutional changes, 42 per cent countries have some form of a coordinating mechanism and 46 per cent have enacted maritime related legislation. There is, however, widespread inability to implement the IM strategy as an 'integrated' whole that balances the overall interests of the nation in the short and long term. Amongst other reasons, IM raises apprehensions over turf, distribution of authority, responsibility and power within the nation (Olsen and Christie, 2000).

**Table 2.3: Porters 5Ps and Integrated Management**

| 5Ps | Porters Definition | Integrated Management Strategy |
|---|---|---|
| **Plan** | Some sort of consciously intended course of action establish direction for the organization | * Integrate all relevant policy areas, sectors and levels of administration.<br>* Land-Sea interface.<br>* Take a short-term and long-term. |
| **Ploy** | A specific maneuver to gain advantage placing the process of strategy formation in its most dynamic setting. | An imposed Integrated Management strategy works as a ploy for overcoming inertia to change and tunnel vision in sectoral organization. |
| **Pattern** | A notion of convergence in a stream of actions-achievement of consistency in organization behaviour. | * Taking a wide-ranging view of inter related problems.<br>* Making knowledgeable decisions based on data and information.<br>* Working with natural forces. Allowing for unforeseen future developments.<br>* Make use of a range of instruments. |
| **Position** | A match between organization and the environment locating the organization within the environment. A match between the internal and external environment-locating the organization in the external environment. | * Concept comprehensiveness-measured along the dimensions of time, space, actors and issues.<br>* Process aggregation-Evaluating the strategy from an overall perspective necessitating weighing interests and setting priorities at each level of management.<br>* Consistent practice- Vertical and horizontal dimension where vertical aspect refers to the accord between the different strategy levels and only one strategy for a given issue is being pursued along the horizontal dimension. |
| **Perspective** | Strategy is a concept, perspective is shared-intention and behaviour in a collective context looks inside the organization-not just a chosen position but an ingrained way of perceiving the world. | * Taking a long term view.<br>* Adopting a process of adaptive management.<br>* Organizing around an integrated approach.<br>* Promoting participation and a collaborative culture.<br>* Developing understanding through interdisciplinary training. |

On the contrary, IM is aimed at being a flexible and transparent planning process that respects existing divisions of authority and does not abrogate or derogate responsibilities of line ministries/departments/agencies in the maritime sector. What an IM strategy requires is a shift in mindsets to a new way of thinking, oriented towards taking a more holistic approach to understanding the interrelationships of economic development, environment protection and protective security in the maritime zone, through an interdisciplinary and intersectoral approach. Multiple polices, due to lack of sufficient convergence between the planning frameworks of the different maritime sectors, risk duplication, conflict, wastage of administrative and intellectual resources, and greater financial costs. IM must therefore be viewed as a comprehensive planning technique that reduces user conflict and ensures policy consistency. It is but one element of a national maritime strategy in the nation's realisation of its maritime power. The other elements of a national maritime strategy include an institutional framework for policy coordination at the international, national, state and local level; legislative mechanism for policy coherence with international norms and national objectives; and a regulatory arrangement for policy compliance across all levels of implementation. The outcome of the national maritime strategy in fulfilling the prime objective of sea power, that is the power to govern the sea, depends on establishing a 'language of change' that all stakeholders can speak and understand.

According to Underdal (1980) "integrated" in IM, means to unify - to put parts together into a whole. There are two generic ways of achieving integration; the direct method, which may be viewed as a 'top-down' approach and the indirect method, which may be viewed as a 'top-down' and 'bottom-up' approach. The direct method seeks to achieve integration across the maritime sectors by defining national policy goals derived from global principles that are to be followed by all government agencies involved in the management of the maritime affairs. The indirect method involves an intellectual strategy and an institutional strategy. The intellectual strategy seeks integration through initiating research, training, and socialisation aimed at developing a more comprehensive and holistic perspective on the part of decision-makers. Both, for the direct method to develop a planning framework for a national policy and the intellectual strategy to be truly representative of all the stakeholders, will require some degree of institutional change. The institutional strategy in itself involves some type of organisational change that facilitates moving issues upwards from the site to the national level and transferring issues from a narrow single sector to a broader multiple sector perspective. Thus, it can be said that, irrespective of the approach at the national level, designing an IM institutional framework that can facilitate putting IM concept into practice, is essential.

There is a need to facilitate universal logic or 'reason' in the way of decision taking, by government officials and scientific experts and, by the community (Visser, 1999). Effective management is really a question of proper institutional design, finding the right balance between national, state and local control in order to achieve the collective and sometimes conflicting goals of different programmes (Elmore, 1985 in Imperial, 1999). The first priority is to create a formalised institutional framework that has the mandate, the human and financial resources and the political will to put into practice the concept of IM (Olsen *etal.*, 1997) (Figure 2.3).

Figure 2.3: Ordering Ocean Governance outcomes

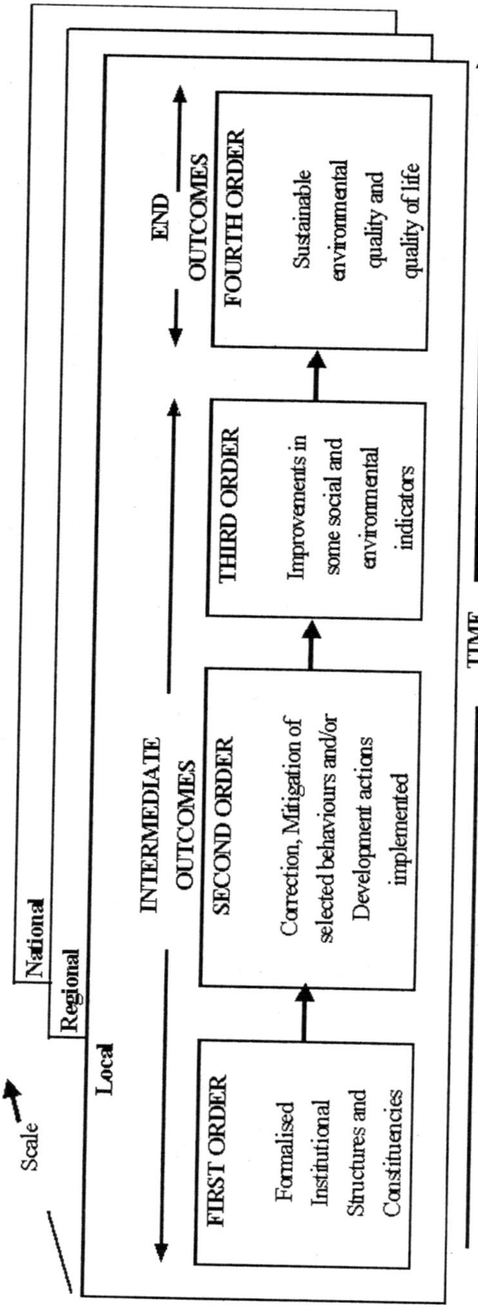


*Source*: Olsen, 1997

In the initiative undertaken by the Association of South East Asian Nations (ASEAN) 'institutional and organisational arrangements were imperative in carrying out the projects and programmes' (Thia-Eng, 1993). In the Netherlands too, it was considered necessary to build an organisational structure for the relevant participants to communicate about problems and solutions (Alphen, 1995). 'The challenge lies in developing practices and institutions that are consistent with the principles we recognise as right, but whose implementation is difficult' (Freidheim, 2000). Limitations in institutional capacities contribute the main barrier to improved resource planning and management (Noble, 2000).

Using the process in IUCN Marine Protection Area (MPA) programme and the writings of Cicin-Sain and Knecht (1998), strengthened by the works of Christie (1997), Clark (1998), Olsen (1997) and Sorensen (1993), the IMs core process needed to develop an institutional framework can be defined (Figure 2.4). The IM core process facilitates design of sustainable policies, plans, programmes and projects for the maritime zone. A policy may be defined as an inspiration and guidance for action, a plan as a set of co-ordinated and timed objectives for the implementation of the policy, and a programme as a set of projects in a particular area (Wood, 1991 in Glasson *et al.,* 1996). Thus, policy provides a framework for the establishment of plans; plans, in turn provide framework for programmes and programmes lead to projects (Table 2.4).

Figure 2.4: IM Core Process

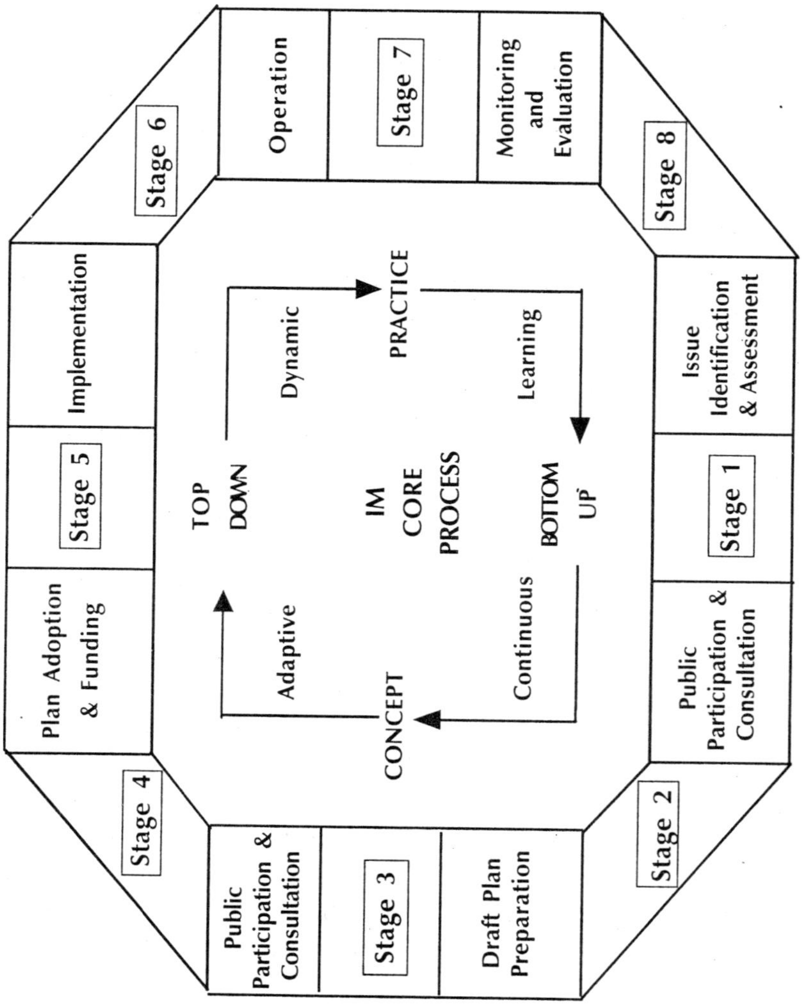

Table 2.4 IM Policy Plan Programme Project Implementation

| Port Strategy | Policy | Plan | Programme | Project |
|---|---|---|---|---|
| National → State → District → Local | National Port Policy → | State Port Plan → | 20 Year Port Building Programme → | Construction of Port |
| | National Policy → | State Strategic Plan → | District Investment Programme → | Local Infrastructure Project |
| | Takes into account cummulative impacts of global changes → | Integrates Security, Environment and Development Decision Making → | Allows for more effective mitigation before a decision is taken → | Strengthens Project Strategic Impact Assessment |

For instance, a national port policy that takes into account the cumulative impacts of global change facilitates a state level strategic plan that integrates the tenets of economic development, environmental protection and maritime security. The investment for the 20 year port building programme benefits from more effective mitigation before a decision is taken at the district level. This strengthens project visibility and long term use at the grass root or local level. In effect, the approach provides for a systematic and comprehensive process of evaluating the impact of national policy, state plan and district programme, consider alternatives, arrive at findings and use the findings in publicly accountable decision making for project implementation at the local level.

## Institutional Framework Design

In a dynamic and complex environment, IM is a concept that can result in a successful adaptive management strategy for sustainable development of the maritime zone. An institutional framework that allows for such a cross-functional IM core process, 'top-down' direction setting and 'bottom-up' issue identification and resolution approach can result in the implementation of a successful IM strategy. The institutional framework has to be based on an analysis of the particular social, economic, cultural and political setting of a nation (Cicin-Sain and Knecht, 1998). There are no 'best or 'right' solutions. The framework cannot be constructed (nor dismantled) overnight because of the underlying cultural ideas and power relationships within an organisation (Visser, 1999). Dealing with the issues requires vision, leadership and courage (Olsen and Christie, 2000). Sustainability depends on co-operation between the different stakeholders, including government officials, scientists and community and, the aggregation of their interests for the long-term access and use of the maritime zone. The involvement of all the stakeholders does not have to mean there is a net loss in power at higher levels in the governance hierarchy (Olsen and Christie, 2000). Every nation based on its social, economic, cultural and political compulsions will need to develop its very own institutional framework for implementation. The United Nations perspective on an institutional design at the national level for the Integrated Management of maritime affairs includes:

a) A Political level consisting of a "Board of Ministers for the Ocean" which could be advised by a multi-stakeholder advisory council.

b) A Bureaucratic level consisting of an "Inter-Ministerial Commission for the Ocean" composed of senior ministry officials.

c) Wide participation and an effective decision making system linking government, scientists, industry and the people.

## Turning Point

The management of the maritime zone is multidisciplinary in nature, balancing economic activity, social equity and environmental quality for sustainable development. Security is an essential precondition to sustainable development. Given the importance of ocean resources, in today's complex economy the management of maritime affairs is of strategic importance to all nations.

The first priority is to create a formalised institutional framework. An institutional framework that allows for cross-functional Integrated Management (IM) core process involving 'top-down' direction setting and 'bottom-up' issue identification and resolution approach can result in the implementation of a successful IM strategy. The United Nations' perspective on an institutional design at the national level for the integrated management of maritime affairs includes political and bureaucratic levels, and lays emphasis on wider participation and an effective decision making system linking government, scientists, industry and the people in general. Based on its social, economic, cultural and political compulsions, nations will need to develop their very own institutional framework for implementation.

# 3

# L'affaire Maritime:

## Repositioning India as a Maritime Nation

India is the largest democracy in the world, seventh largest country, the second most populous, one of the fastest emerging economy, and has the tenth largest Exclusive Economic Zone. The country is home to more than one billion people, of which about 250 million people live near the coast. The 21$^{st}$ century could well belong to India if it were to utilise its resources in a sustainable manner and reposition itself as a maritime nation. India has had long distance seaborne trade, westwards with the Red Sea, Egypt, and East African Coast, and Eastwards with SE Asia and Indo-China. This was well established long before European navigators found their way into the area in the 15$^{th}$ century. As early as the 5$^{th}$ century BC, the Nandas' enjoyed supremacy at sea. They were succeeded by the Mauryas. The age of the Mauryans witnessed considerable maritime activity between the Indians and the house of Selucus. Even the records of Alexander's campaign show considerable maritime activity. It was on the way back to Greece, that Alexander dispatched Admiral Nearchus to sail from the mouth of the Indus to the Euphrates. Indeed, the emissaries dispatched by emperor Ashoka to spread his message of Buddhism also used the same route.

The Andhra-Kushana period, from the 2nd century BC to the 3rd century AD, saw the discovery of the monsoon winds that shortened the long and tedious coastal passage. The discovery of the "trade winds" as they came to be known opened new vistas in oceanic navigation and brought about a volumetric growth of seaborne trade. Political relations between India and the Roman Empire developed along with booming trade that lasted till the fall of the Andhra Empire in 217 AD.

The period of the Gupta's too saw considerable maritime activity. The opening of ports in Dwarka, Porbander, Veraval and Cambay saw a shift in the dominance of the South as regards to oceanic trade. The conquest of Bengal as described by Kalidasa's *Raghuvansa*, was accomplished under the protection of a naval fleet. Progress in astronomy and the discovery of the magnetic compass or "Matsya Yantra" were attributed to this period. The reign of Harshavardhana saw the exchange of diplomatic relations and trade between India and China. The first wave of immigrants from Gujarat to Java set off in the 6th century. However, the first naval exploits of the Indian seafarers supposedly occurred in 712 AD when Dahar, the King of Sind crushed the seaborne campaign sent by the Caliph of Iraq aimed at Debal, the seaport in Sind. Subsequent invasions by the Arbas in 756 AD and 776 AD were also repulsed decisively by the Saindhavas.

In the South, the Pallavas succeeded the Satavahana dynasty and took over the command of the seas. The Pallava's maintained a strong naval force and mounted successful naval campaigns against Ceylon until 9th century AD. The Chalukya's who reigned in the same period also boasted of a powerful Navy. It was Pulakesin II who went on to build a formidable empire with a long seaboard that facilitated all oceanic enterprises. The greatest of all maritime kingdoms of India were the Cholas in the South. Having set up ports with excellent administrative facilities all over the coastline, the Cholas backed by a formidable Army and Navy carried out thriving trade with the West. Coming into existence in 1336 AD, the Vijaynagar Empire was spread over Mysore, Kanara and the whole of South India. This period saw great shipbuilding activity and maritime trade with the Burmese, Thais, Chinese, Indonesians, Arabs, Persians, Abbyssinians and later even the Portuguese. However, the advent of the Portuguese, who in 1510 annexed Goa, and the incessant wars with the Deccan sultanates, led to the decline and final eclipse of the Vijayanagar Empire.

India, one of the bronze age civilisations symbolised by populous cities, highly skilled industries, far-flung commerce and a pictographic script was a country of wealth and prosperity. India engaged in regular and extensive trade and even reached the markets of the Tigris and Euphrates. Tin, gold and precious stones were brought from other countries and fish was brought from the Arabian Sea to augment food supplies. The Indian subcontinent held an unchallenged monopoly on overseas commerce in the entire Indian Ocean, until the advent of the Arabs in 2$^{nd}$ century AD. One of the main reasons for our decline was the complete lack of appreciation to use naval power to aid inland battles fought in areas contiguous to the sea.

Indians came to accept Arab seafarers as middlemen in their overseas trade with the West. This exclusive status was exploited by the Arabs to generate heavy profits, thereby exasperating the West. The capture of

Constantinople - which had been a vital link between East and West, between Asia and Europe - by the Ottoman Turks in 1453, blocked the principal lines of communication of the East-West trade. This necessitated finding a sea route to India by the Europeans. Why did Europeans venture in search of new trade routes and not Asians? This was because the manufacturing and commercial activity of India and even China and the East far surpassed that of the West. Europe wanted Chinese silk, porcelain, precious stones, spices - pepper, cloves, nutmeg, cinnamon and ginger - and Indian ivory, pearls, jewellery, precious woods, and the finest muslins and calicoes.

The first European nation to find a sea route to India was Portugal, when Vasco-da-Gama on 11 May 1498, reached Calicut. Sea Power thus changed the face of world geopolitics, for the year 1500 was subsequently chosen by historians to mark the divide between modern and pre-modern times. A study of India's maritime history thus reveals that they reigned supreme over the Indian Ocean from very early times to the 13$^{th}$ century AD. India took to the sea for commercial purposes rather than political. Evidences from sources other than the Vedas show that maritime trade existed from the 6$^{th}$ century BC. The Bible too refers to merchandise from ports of South India finding their way to King Solomon's territories.

## Geography

India is the geographical fulcrum of the Indian Ocean. Nehru referred to it as, "The pivot of Asia." As the seventh largest country in the world, India is Asia's second largest nation. It has a landmass of 3,287,263 km$^2$ with a land frontier of 15,200 km comprising 22 of the 35

States and Union Territories (UTs). The maritime frontier of India is more difficult to define as it extends from the sea across the land-sea interface to an inland limit. Although, India is divided into four physio-geographic zones, the Northern Mountains, Great Plains, Deccan Plateau and Coastal Plains and Islands - to obviate the physio-geographic anomalies such as the Orissa Highlands touching the coastline being part of the Deccan Plateau and the Sunderbans in West Bengal being part of the Northern Plains, and also to ease the management process, the inland limit of the maritime frontier are defined by the individual States and Union Territories (UTs) administrative boundary. As a consequence, the 13 coastal states/UTs with a total coastline of 7,516.6 km together have a land area of 1,396,540 sq km$^2$ and a population of 489,581,033 million (Appendix 3). Thus, the inland limit of India's maritime frontier covers 42.48 per cent of the country's area and 47.67 per cent of the country's population with an average population density of 350 against the national average of 313. The ocean space of India's maritime frontier includes 155,889 km$^2$ of territorial seas, an Exclusive Economic Zone (EEZ) of 2,013,410 km$^2$, a deep sea mining area of 75,000 km$^2$ (another 75,000 km$^2$ handed over to the International Seabed authority under the agreement of Pioneer investor), 1197 island territories and a continental shelf that is yet to be claimed of at the least 530,000 km$^2$, if not more. India has signed maritime border agreements with Myanmar, Thailand, Malaysia, Indonesia and Sri Lanka (Appendix 3). The delimitation of maritime boundaries with Bangladesh and Pakistan must await the settlement of disputes over New Moore Island and Sir Creek respectively. With the historic and geographic backdrop, an appraisal of the pressures of economic development, environmental protection, and maritime security, as also the government's response is central to the understanding India's maritime dimension.

## Pressures of Economic Development

India is one of the ten most industrialised countries in the world, and the eighth largest economy. During the period 1992 to 1997, it has grown by an average of 6.68 per cent. The ninth five-year plan (1997-2002) was expected to set the stage for growth in the post plan period that could be as high as 7.7 percent. During the ninth plan India achieved 5.35 per cent growth rate despite a slow-down in the world economy, weather related shocks, natural disasters, - cyclone in Orissa, earthquake in Gujarat - and the Kargil conflict. The tenth five-year plan (2002-2007) identifies 8 per cent growth rate as feasible. The targeted 8 per cent growth rate can be achieved if sufficient political will is mobilised to identify efficiency enhancing polices both at the macro level and also at the sectoral level involving a radical break from past practices and institutional arrangements. The five coastal states of Tamil Nadu, Maharashtra, Gujarat, Andhra and Karnataka account for two-thirds of export oriented businesses in the country.

## Shipping and Ports

The 12 major ports and 61 reportedly operable of the 185 notified non-major ports along India's long coastline together handled 418.27 million tonnes of cargo traffic in 2002-03. While the major ports handled 313.45 million tonnes, the remaining 104.82 million tonnes was handled by the non-major ports. Despite the increase in trade flows - 90 per cent by volume and 77 per cent by value - Indian ports continue to show lower productivity in comparison to other ports in the Asian region. India's export led growth will require substantial addition in infrastructure and port productivity to handle the increased volume of trade. Indian shipping, which is ranked 21$^{st}$ in the world (17$^{th}$ until 2001) constitutes just 1.04 per cent of world shipping tonnage and carries only 17 per cent of India's trade by volume. With 618 registered vessels of 6.43 million GRT, only 25 per cent of Indian shipping is below nine years, 41 per cent between 10 to 19 years and nearly 35 per cent over 20 years as compared to the global average of 18 years. Overall, 60 per cent of India's shipping fleet needs to be replaced in the next five years.

## Oil and Gas

India's growing dependence on the sea is underlined by its energy demand for crude oil. India imports 70 per cent of its crude oil requirement, nearly two-thirds of which comes from the Persian Gulf. While domestic onshore production meets 10 per cent of the requirement, the balance 20 per cent comes from offshore production. Thus, nearly 2/3rd of India's oil production is from the offshore region and contributes over Rs 42,000 crores to the national economy. India's total sedimentary area equals 3.14 million Km$^2$ of which only 17 per cent or 0.535 million Km$^2$ is moderately to well explored. Presently, of the Petroleum Exploration Licence (PEL) areas under operation, 72.3 per cent of the areas are offshore (Western Offshore - 49.51 per cent and Eastern offshore - 22.79 per cent) and 10 per cent in the coastal states of Andhra Pradesh (4.58 per cent), Gujarat (2.68 per cent), West Bengal (1.34 per cent), Orissa (0.77 per cent) and Tamil Nadu (0.63 per cent). Similarly, of the Mining Licence (ML) areas under operation, 42.3 per cent of the areas are offshore (Western Offshore

- 39.33 per cent and Easter offshore - 2.97 per cent) and 29.38 per cent in the coastal states of Gujarat (Cambay Basin - 25.47 per cent), Andhra Pradesh (Krishna- Godavari Basin -2.21 per cent) and Tamil Nadu (Cauvery Basin - 1.70 per cent).

## Minerals

Taking into consideration the projected growth in industrial development, there will be increasing demands for metals such as copper, nickel, cobalt and silver besides gold and platinum group of metals. For example, India's current per capita consumption of copper is 0.11 kg as compared to 7.7 kg for the industrialised nations and 3.0-kg as a world average. Current domestic supplies in terms of terrestrial mineral resources of some metals are inadequate. India has no known deposits of cobalt, and nickel deposits are a meagre 137mt compared to Canada's 8,600mt. (Roonwal, 1996 in Qasim & Roonwal, 1996). On the other hand, the mineral potential within the Indian EEZ is considerable. Increasing pressures on land for agriculture, human settlement and industry will require the development of the Exclusive Economic Zone as an integral part of the country's socio-economic growth. Under its mining programme, India as a pioneer investor in deep-sea mining has successfully tested a prototype for mineral extraction up to 400m depth. Besides, according to Bureau of Mines estimates, over 55 percent of the total area under mining leases is in the coastal states (Table 3.1).

**Table 3.1: Coastal State-wise Mining Leases**

| Sl. No. | State | No. of leases | Leasearea (hect.) |
|---|---|---|---|
| 1 | Andhra Pradesh | 1707 | 56459.11 |
| 2 | Goa | 395 | 30304.63 |
| 3 | Gujarat | 1428 | 31310.50 |
| 4 | Karnataka | 610 | 72153.39 |
| 5 | Kerala | 114 | 2394.54 |
| 6 | Maharashtra | 234 | 17587.28 |
| 7 | Orissa | 605 | 99087.74 |
| 8 | Tamil Nadu | 669 | 43980.01 |
| 9 | West Bengal | 76 | 12420.76 |
| 10 | Total | 5838 | 365697.96 |

*Source:* Indian Bureau of Mines (http://imb.nic.in)

## Fisheries

India is the third largest producer of fish in the world and second in inland fish production. Nearly 6.7 million people depend on fishing as their sole means of livelihood and the fisheries sector provides employment to nearly 36 million people or 15 per cent of the coastal population. The annual potential yield in the EEZ has been assessed to be 3.934 million tonnes. The present level of marine fish exploitation is around 2.8 million tonnes. In the absence of a deep-sea fishing policy, the waters up to 100 m depth are subject to intense fishing pressure. Marine fish production has reached a plateau and even with the slow growth of 2.19 per cent per annum is showing signs of overexploitation. Exports of sea food products have exceeded US$1.4 billion in 2001, and could be greatly expanded by deep sea fishing with marine fish production touching 3.5 million tonnes. The challenge lies in developing a policy that promotes deep-sea fishing and yet safeguards the interests of coastal fishermen. Fish, which has a significant quality for processing, has very poor value addition in India. The value of fish in Japan, which has less than half of the produce of India, is US$ 4.37 per kg as compared to US$ 1.11 per kg of India. Post harvest processing and marketing are the weakest link in the chain of Indian exports and domestic value of fish.

## Tourism

Although tourism to India accounts for only 0.67 per cent of the world's tourism market, it is the second largest foreign exchange earner in the country bringing nearly US$3.042 billion in foreign exchange. Nearly, 53 per cent of the 2.5 million tourists visit tourist spots in the coastal states/UTs each year. India's beaches with their mesmerising beauty and calm provide an ideal getaway for those looking for solitude amidst the serenity of nature. The principal constraints facing the tourism sector is lack of adequate infrastructure support - transportation (inland waterways, ports, airports, road, rail), accommodation, quality of facilities and services - poor quality of the environment surrounding the tourist sites, and the security scenario in the region affecting the perception of India as a safe and secure destination. Tourism is a classic example of the interdependence and indivisibility of economic development, environment protection and maritime security for the coastal states and UTs, especially the island territories. The main internal threats to development of tourism are security, safety, health situation; failure to involve local communities in the decision making process;

and the failure to adopt and implement sustainable development and management principles and practices. At the institutional level, it requires a framework which is government-led, private sector-driven and community welfare-oriented.

## Project Development and Implementation

Vast stretches of land along the Indian coastline is still pristine in nature. However, project development is viewed in an isolated manner where the cost-benefit analysis only looks at the economic gains. The social, human, and ecology aspects are not rated in the cost benefit analysis. There exists a piecemeal approach to management with each department making its own laws. For example, the port area cannot be subject to any other law other than that of the Port Management Authority. The Public Works Department does not consider other impacts of coast protection measures. Similarly, the State Ministry of Environment has little influence over the State Housing Board responsible for domestic sewage disposal.

A review of centrally managed major national projects undertaken by the Department of Programme Implementation (DPI) identified factors responsible for poor rate of project implementation to be: inadequate field investigation; lack of adequate data; inadequate analysis of environmental and rehabilitation implications; delays in clearance from various regulatory agencies for land acquisition and procurement of materials; poor project co-ordination and planning; changes in the scope of a project midway through execution; and inability of project managers to take prompt decisions on various aspects of these projects.

## Pressure of Environmental Protection

### Conservation

India contains a great wealth of biological diversity in its forests, its wetlands and in its marine areas. Evergreen tropical rain forests are found in the Andaman and Nicobar Islands and the Western Ghats on the West Coast. Small remnants of rain forest are found in Orissa on the East Coast. The Western Ghats covering an estimated area of 159,000 $km^2$ is an area of exceptional biological diversity and a region of great conservation concern. There are currently seven national parks in the Western Ghats with a total area of 2,073 $km^2$ (equivalent to 1.3 per cent of the region) and 39 wildlife sanctuaries covering an area of about 13,862 $km^2$ (8.1 per cent).

India ranks $14^{th}$ amongst the 22 countries that contain the world's major mangrove areas. The northern Bay of Bengal, the Sunderbans, and the Ganges delta support over 500,000 hectares. The Sunderbans make up the single largest contiguous block of mangrove forests in the world, with 40 per cent of the area within India. Under the World Heritage Convention, five natural sites have been inscribed as areas of 'outstanding universal value' of which Sunderbans National Park (West Bengal) is on the East Coast. The total floral diversity of the Sunderbans amounts to some 330 species. In the Andaman and Nicobar, mangroves total about 115,200 hectares, and much of this is relatively pristine. There is a rich variety of wetland habitats with about 3,900,000 hectares of estuarine wetlands. The total area of wetlands (excluding rivers) in India is 58,286,000 hectares, i.e. 18.4 per cent of the country. Under the Ramsar Convention, India has six sites covering some 192,973 hectares of important wetlands and includes Chilka Lake (Orissa) on the East Coast.

The Gulf of Kachchh in Gujarat has some of the most northerly reefs in the world. Besides Palk Bay and Gulf of Mannar in Tamil Nadu, the Andaman and Nicobar Islands and Lakshadweep Islands are the other coral reef areas. The Gulf of Mannar (Tamil Nadu) and Wandoor (Andaman) have been declared as Marine National Parks and Malvan coast (Maharashtra), Gulf of Kachchh (Gujarat), Jamnagar (Gujarat) as Marine Sanctuaries because of their high biodiversity. There are a number of other specialised ecosystems such as Pulicat Lake (Tamil Nadu) and Point Calimere (Tamil Nadu), which exhibit a large variety of marine life.

The Indian Forest Act 1927; Forest (Conservation) Act 1980; National Forest Policy 1988; Wildlife (Protection) Act 1972; Environmental (Protection) Act 1986; Coastal Zone Regulation Act 1992; and Coastal Zone Management Plans of the state government are legal tools which are applicable for protection and conservation of the Marine Protected Areas (MPAs) and regulation of the activities in the area. Maritime and Port Policy and the Port Act of states are the other legal aspects, which are used for development of ports and harbours. It has been observed that the Forest (Conservation) Act of 1980, the Wildlife (Protection) Act of 1972 and the Port Act of the states have contradictory provisions, which result in conflicts between the departments.

The Coast Regulation Zone (CRZ) Act was enacted to protect the Indian coast from degradation. The area influenced by tidal action upto 500m from High Tide Line (HTL) and the land between the Low Tide Line (LTL) and the HTL has been declared as Coastal Regulation Zone (CRZ). Recently state governments are requesting the Union to consider revision of the CRZ. There is a clear need for synergy in legislation and action to prevent degradation of the coastal habitat. Critical to conservation is the 5,318.9 $Km^2$ of MPA by way of nine marine national parks covering an area of 2181.8 $Km^2$ and 17 marine sanctuaries that cover an area of 3137.2 $Km^2$ under the Wildlife (Protection) Act, 1972. The 26 MPAs cover only 13.2 percent of the total coastal wetlands in the country.

## Waste Disposal

Currently, more than 90 per cent of the pollutants generated end up in the coastal zone. Demographic pressure in the urban cities and towns has resulted in the production of enormous amounts of domestic waste materials. Domestic sewage contributes to the largest amount of waste with four billion $m^3$ of waste reaching the coastal environment. Domestic wastes are discharged mostly in untreated condition due to the lack of treatment facilities in most of the cities and towns. Major industrial cities and towns of the country such as Surat, Mumbai, Kochi, Chennai, Vishakhapatnam, and Kolkota are situated on or near the coastline. The total quantity of industrial waste generated is estimated to be 40 million $m^3$. India being an agricultural country uses large quantities of fertilisers and pesticides to sustain its agricultural production. About 50 million $m^3$ of river-borne effluents, 33 million tons of land wastes and five million tons of fertiliser residues are discharged into the coastal and marine environment. A nation-wide marine pollution-monitoring programme operating for the last 10 years has identified areas of clean sea. It has been found that the sea beyond two km, all along the coast, except in Mumbai, is clean. In case of Mumbai, the sea beyond five km is clean.

## Coastal Engineering

Coastal engineering studies have revealed that the construction of breakwaters alter the sediment transport mechanism in the coastal areas, thereby causing erosion and accretion, depending on the direction of the littoral drift. Such impacts have already been noticed due to construction of ports of Chennai and Paradip. It has been found that due to the establishment of Chennai port, an accretion of 75 acres occurred in the last 60 years south of the port, as well as severe erosion in the north resulting in the loss of 83 acres of land. The navigational channel from Bay of Bengal to the Hooghly estuary (Kolkota and Haldia are two inland, major, ports in India) is causing severe erosion problems in Saugar and Niachara islands. The cyclonic weather, which is common along the East Coast (175 cyclones in the last 100 years) also, causes erosion problems. In Tamil Nadu, about 80 km of coastline, in Orissa about 30-40 km of coastline and in West Bengal about 180 km of coastline are affected (Ramachandran, 1999 in Salomons, 1999). Serious coastal erosion problems are also experienced in the western states of Karnataka and Kerala due to intense monsoon activity. In Karnataka, nearly 0.2 metric ton of sand material is lost per year due to monsoons and resultant sand drift affecting 73 km of the coastline. In Kerala nearly 80 per cent (about 400 km of the 530 km coastline) is experiencing coastal erosion (Ramachandran, 1999 in Salomons, 1999).

It is not surprising, therefore, that India's rapid industrial, population and economic growth is causing severe environmental degradation and pollution problems with local, regional and national impacts. Population pressure and urbanisation are responsible for deforestation due to destruction of forests through increasing use of fuel-wood, encroachment of forestland for cultivation and re-appropriation of forestland for townships (Pernetta, 1993). Industrialisation and a growing demand for consumer goods places greater pressure for the extraction, procurement, and conversion of natural resources. Infrastructure development such as mines, roads, ports, dams and canal constructions have also resulted in the degradation of the coastal and marine biodiversity (Pernetta, 1993). Whilst such development provides employment opportunities, it also leads to increased inward migration which compounds existing problems. With the success of economic growth, India has simultaneously witnessed a significant deterioration in the quality of its air, water, and soil. Major contributors to air pollution problems in India include thermal power stations, industrial factories, vehicles, and the use of non-commercial fuels such as coal briquettes, animal dung, and trash by large sections of the population. The negative environmental effects from increased fossil fuel use will likely increase as India seeks to meet the energy demands of its expanding economy. Most of the rivers, streams, and large stretches of the coastal and marine environment in India are highly polluted with municipal waste, waste generated from industry, chemical agents from fertilisers, pesticides from crop protection, and silt from degraded catchments. Although there is a Coastal Regulation Zone Notification designed to protect the coastal and marine ecosystems, implementation is weak and marine pollution continues largely unabated. The Planning Commission of India identified growing population, urbanisation, changing agricultural, industrial and water resource management amongst the issues that have resulted in perceptible deterioration in the quality and sustainability of the environment.

## Pressures of Maritime Security

Security is important to the maritime economic development agenda. Resource decline, unsustainable development and environmental degradation are linked to security in a number of ways. It is submitted here that 'security' has to be understood not simply in terms of the potential for (or absence of) conflict or interstate tension, but in human, and environment security terms. A human security paradigm focuses concern on increased social tensions and political instabilities within states because of terrorism, insurgency, piracy, drug trafficking and maritime fraud. Some of the environment security concerns are trans-boundary air pollution and acid rain, degradation of river ecosystems, potential for conflict over water as a shared trans-boundary resource, oil spills and tensions over maritime pollution. Finally, traditional security would take the form of maritime sovereignty and safeguarding infrastructure development in the maritime zone.

It is no longer adequate to focus only on the traditional military threats to maritime security. Further, the non-military dimension of national security - piracy, terrorism, drug trafficking and narcotics, illegal immigration, environmental security, human security, - has become inseparable from international security and would increasingly co-exist with the traditional military dimension of a nation's security concerns. Added to that, ever since the 11 september 2001 attacks on America, the spectre of maritime terrorism has become real. The terrorist attack on the French super-tanker Limburg in Yemen on 06 October 2002, the attack on an Israeli warship on 24 November 2002 are the beginnings of maritime oriented terrorism threats to national security. Maritime terrorism can take many guises and can have catastrophic consequences on a nation's economic and environmental security. The nature of maritime transportation which is founded on the principles of "Freedom of Navigation" allows foreign ships to hug the Indian coastline without having to report their position, nature of cargo and composition of crew. The potential threats from these ships includes hijacking and blowing up of a super tanker off the Indian coastline to use of biological, chemical, nuclear and radiological weapons of mass destruction in one or more of our major ports. There are nearly 16000 calls made annually by ships at the 12 major ports. In 2002-03, nearly 3.3 million containers were loaded/unloaded at these ports. One of the security concerns is that a negligible percentage of these containers are inspected to verify the natures and type of cargo.

Some could argue that non-military threats should be the concern of law enforcers, economists, environmentalists, lawyers, and scientists rather than strategists. This is not so; the classic diplomatic, military and policing trinity put forward by Ken Booth is largely a function of navies and naval power. Maritime strategists must, therefore, take into consideration all factors that have political, legal, technological, economic, environmental and social implications. Today, sea power, i.e. the power to govern the sea, and, thus, maritime strategy, requires nations to synthesise their political, legal, diplomatic and operational responses in the management of their maritime zone. India's concept of sea power is highly fragmented and suffers from lack of coordination amongst the multitude of ministries and departments - Ministries of Defence, Home, External Affairs, Petroleum and Natural Gas, and Shipping, State Governments, Police, Customs, DG Shipping, Maritime Boards, Fisheries Departments, Port Authorities, Central Industrial Security Force (CISF), Border Security Force (BSF),

Coast Guard, and Navy - attempting protective security in the maritime zone. As a consequence, the 7516.6 km coastline is a very porous border.

The principal sea-going forces are the Navy and the Coast Guard. It was in the backdrop of large-scale smuggling that the Government of India (GoI) created the Coast Guard in 1978, as a new service to undertake law enforcement in waters under national jurisdiction and ensure safety of life and property at sea. The Coast Guard, thus, emerged as an independent force for general superintendence and policing, driven largely by the Navy's desire of not wanting to commit "High-value assets for low-end jobs" - for better or for worse the phrase is frequently used even today by the Navy and exploited by the Coast Guard to its advantage. Why advantage Coast Guard? This is so because as the Indian Coast Guard attempts to model itself around the US Coast Guard ($10^{th}$ largest Navy in the world), there is duplication in its roles and functions with that of the Indian Navy. The Indian Coast Guard, created to operate along the coastline in geographic areas of national jurisdiction, is now moving into the diplomatic realm of Navy as it begins to undertake overseas deployments.

The utility of a Coast Guard as a seaward police force for law enforcement, environment protection and safety of life and property at sea is unquestionable and the requirement is only going to increase. However, the concept has ingrained failings due to lack of clarity all round on the roles/functions that need to be performed by the Coast Guard and by the Navy in an effort to optimise utilisation of assets and minimise costs. This has now become increasingly evident from the fact that the Ministry of Home Affairs is debating setting up a separate coastal police force for law enforcement functions in the territorial seas (12 nm) to be supplemented by the Coast Guard. The Customs and Excise Board under the Ministry of Finance is aiming to strengthen its Customs Marine Wing to operate independent of the Coast Guard to prevent smuggling, and enforce the immigration, fiscal and sanitary laws in the Contiguous Zone (24 nm). Ironically, the Ministry of Shipping has nominated DG Shipping as the implementing agency for the International Ship and Port Facility Security (ISPS) Code and Indian ports are proceeding to implement the provisions of the ISPS Code principally through the CISF with waterfront security being undertaken independent of the Coast Guard. Ideally protecting the country's economic resources at sea should be a single agency function. Yet, the critical offshore defence and security structure is less than ideal. The Government of India (GoI) has recently constituted an "Advisor to GoI on Offshore Defence and Security" under the Indian Navy. At the same time, the Ministry of Petroleum and Natural Gas has an "Offshore Security Coordination Committee" under the Coast Guard.

## Impact on Maritime Affairs

The matrix of cause and consequence between economic development, environmental protection and maritime security is thus a complex one. Economic development driving environmental degradation can result in actual or possible conflict between and within countries over the resultant scarcity of resources. On the other hand, inequitable distribution of resources and environmental degradation due to infrastructure development can create a space for sub-state actors to further their cause by increasing social tensions and political instabilities through the propagation of conflict. There exists the potential for conflict over water as a shared transboundary resource within a nation and between nations. While the access to marine resources where sovereignty claims overlap or are in doubt can lead to conflict between nations, and resource scarcity, such as, declining fish stocks can in turn lead to conflict not just between nations but also between coastal or fishing communities within the nation. In November 2003, Kerala Fishermen had burnt down the fishing boats of the fishermen from Tamil Nadu at sea. Besides, growing energy demands and uncertainty over energy supplies can be a motive for controlling the sources of energy leading to conflict. Added to all this, the threat from maritime terrorism, piracy, drug trafficking and narcotics, illegal immigration and crime at sea calls for international cooperation and national responses. The Planning Commission of India concludes that development is not possible with the focus on a single activity underscoring the need for convergence of policy spheres and synergy amongst the facilitators.

## Response

### The Government Structure

A sovereign, socialist, secular, democratic republic, India has a parliamentary system of government with a federal structure (Bhardwaj, 1998 in Kurian, 1998) with a clear division of responsibility. Governance is a constitutional division of power between the Union and State governments, in which the Union plays a major role as a central planner, regulator, investor, manager, and producer. Essentially, all lands, minerals, and other things of value underlying the ocean within the framework of UNCLOS III shall vest in the Union. The resources of the water column have been split two ways in that the resources within the territorial sea vest in the state governments and resources beyond the territorial sea and up to the EEZ vest in the Union. The constitutional and legal framework also provides for a local level through the Panchayat system and the formation of Municipal bodies forming a three-tier governance structure.

Planning in India derives its objectives from directive of state policy enshrined in the Constitution. The Planning Commission set up in 1950, prepares the blue print of development taking an overall view of the needs and resources of the country. The periodic national development plans covering a five year span, reflects the sectoral objectives prepared by line ministries. The Planning Commission undertakes screening against financial and political concerns. The national plan derived from this process tends to set out broad objectives weighted by financial and political constraints and is linked weakly to institutional or procedural changes which could foster sustainable development. India is into its tenth five-year plan (2002-2007), which also does not consider the maritime zone and the activities therein as a whole. In the *Economic Survey* of 2002-2003 the different maritime activities that have been discussed are tourism, oil and gas, fisheries and ports. Tourism, and oil and gas, have been mentioned in the industry chapter, fisheries in the agriculture chapter and ports in the infrastructure chapter. The shipping sector is conspicuously devoid of any mention in this report.

The business of the Government of India is transacted in ministries/departments created by the President on the advice of the Prime Minister under the Government of India (Allocation of Business) Rules, 1961. In 1947, the number of ministries at the Centre was 18. As of now, the government consists of 43 ministries and at least 61 departments indicating a sectoral approach to management. A system of parliamentary standing and ad-hoc committees provides for detailed scrutiny of all legislative and other matters that come up before the parliament. In 1993, 17 departmentally related standing committees were set up to provide parliamentary surveillance over the administration. These are: agriculture; communications; commerce; defence; energy; external affairs; finance; food; civil supplies and public distribution; home affairs; human resource development; industry; labour and welfare; petroleum and chemicals; railways; science and technology; environment and forests; transport and tourism; and, urban and rural development (Bhardwaj, 1998 in Kurian, 1998). By concentrating on long term plans and policies, these committees are in a privileged position to provide direction and guidance necessary for broad policy formulation and achievement of long term national perspective. It becomes evident that the formation of committees is on sectoral lines.

The government has periodically reviewed the relations between the Union and States in the political, economic, financial, and administrative spheres. The past forty-five years of experience reveals that while the force of development has gradually weakened some minor institutional hurdles, the nation has not fully succeeded in building up institutions to answer the need of time. The Planning Commission indicates that past programmes have failed to deliver because of the inadequacies in design and implementation. For example, assumptions have to be made about certain technical and non-technical parameters because of lack of knowledge about the local situation, inadequate database and time and resource constraints. A perennial problem in case of Union sponsored programmes is the application of standard per unit cost in estimating the cost of the programme. On the contrary, project costs vary from region to region because of variations in topography and the unique nature of some regions. Besides, available resources are spread too thinly across a large number of projects leading to sub-optimal project outcome/ cost overruns. The 'top-down' approach in planning and implementation has led to the formulation of schemes without assessing the needs of the people. Programme implementation agencies have been created without the necessary associated institutional changes, leading to implementation by existing departments working independently for different components of a programme. The outcome has been lack of focus, wastage of resources and lack of co-ordination among the line departments. Programme implementation agencies have been created without the necessary associated institutional changes, leading to implementation by existing departments working independently for different components of a programme. The outcome has been lack of focus, wastage of resources and lack of co-ordination among the line departments. Lack of accountability and inadequate allocation of funds to implementation agencies is also identified as a major constraint to successful implementation. A voluntary organisation unearthed several cases of large-scale misappropriation of funds in rural development programmes in four districts of one State. The Planning Commission has attributed this to lack of people's participation in the implementation of programmes, lack of transparency in the operation of the schemes and inadequacy in the monitoring mechanism. Monitoring and evaluation of programmes have failed to apply necessary corrective steps in programme formulation and implementation, as physical and financial indicators do not reflect the actual performance of programmes. Information generated through the monitoring and evaluation system is not analysed with a problem solving perspective. Further, programmes in the social sector are formulated without addressing the question of sustainability of benefits that accrue from the programme. A redundant and ineffective administration has led to inadequacies in planning and implementation resulting in abnormally high costs of some programmes. An underlying financial problem faced by the government is integrating long term planning into short-term annual budgetary process. As a result, there is no proper management of the flow of funds resulting in delays and inadequate funds to implementing agencies. The general approach in implementation is 'top-down' and 'target oriented' without assessing the needs of the people and more concerned with the mere fulfilment of targets assigned.

## Maritime Security Response

In so far as maritime security is concerned, can the Indian polity and bureaucracy deliver? In the face of changing maritime security threats and a fragmented security framework, can our speed and alacrity match the international community? Of immediate concern is controlling the movement of tankers carrying petroleum, natural gas, chemicals, and hazardous materials. India must be able to identify, board, and inspect any vessel that could be used as a weapon of mass destruction against our ports and cities. The core issues are that of accurate information, intelligence, and surveillance of all vessels, cargo, and people, extending up to 200 nm from the Indian coastline. Such awareness provides the key to identifying threats as early and as distant as possible for determining the most effective and optimal course of intervention.

To be able to secure our coastline requires a range of political, operational, legal and industry responses. At the political level, a range of bilateral and multilateral arrangements are needed to share information and intelligence, prohibit sub standard ships and ships that do not adopt adequate security measures from entering the Indian ports. There is a requirement of adopting stringent inspection measures to plug the biggest security hole in movement of cargo containers. Immediate operational responses include a ship monitoring system in the Lakshadweep, and Andaman and Nicobar islands, besides developing comprehensive security plans for each port and positioning port security officers in all the 12 major and 61 operational minor ports in the country, and the creation, training and positioning of response teams to deal with chemical, biological, nuclear and radiological weapons. More importantly, India needs to set up local port security committees to better coordinate the efforts of the intelligence agencies, Customs and Immigration, Indian Navy and Coast Guard, State Police, Central Industrial Security Force (CISF), Port authorities and shipping agencies. India's legal response must be aimed at strengthening national laws and extending jurisdiction of Indian courts to sea areas of national jurisdiction. An industry response includes recognising the need for regulatory measures, an Automatic Identification System on all Indian merchant ships and motor powered fishing boats, positioning trained ship security officers on board their merchant ships and developing ship security plans.

## An Integrated Approach to Response Measures

It is clear that India needs to quickly put into place a mechanism for prevention, interdiction and defense against any form of asymmetric threat across its maritime borders.

India also needs to synergise the trinity of policy spheres - economic development, environmental protection and maritime security. This is possible only through a coordinated effort between the wide spectrum of central government ministries and departments, state government, enforcement agencies and with active participation from the Indian industry, academic and scientific institutions, voluntary organisations and the Panchayati Raj Institutions.

In contrast with the situation on land, where management practices are based on long established laws and institutions, in the oceans the mechanisms to deal with the interdependence and indivisibility of economic development, environmental protection and maritime security are still fairly new and as yet insufficiently tested by time and practical use. Furthermore, on land the jurisdiction of the state can guarantee compliance with the law through strong enforcement mechanisms. The framework for management of the oceans faces the challenge of having to protect a nation's right in its maritime zone while exercising commitment to "Freedom of the Seas" doctrine. These constraints define a special and unique role and responsibility for the nation's government vis-à-vis the challenge of ocean governance. It implies a holistic approach where problems are closely interrelated and must be considered as a whole for an inclusive nature of decision making and implementation. The planning process is said to be evolving from a highly centralised planning system towards indicative planning where the planning commission concerns itself with the building of a long term strategic vision of the future and decides on priorities of the nation. There is realisation that an integrated approach can lead to better results at much lower costs and the Planning Commission is beginning to play such an integrative role in policy formulation of human and economic development. However, an integrated approach to management of maritime affairs is yet to emerge as an agenda for the government.

Simplistically stated, the mainstay of the integrated approach lies in grass-root inputs for policy formulation at the national level and grass-root monitoring of policy implementation at the state level. There is some evidence of a shift in government thinking towards an integrated management from a sectoral management concept. Towards this, the Planning Commission in calling for suitable institutional reforms suggests involvement of non-governmental organisations and participation of the people at the grass roots level in the formulation, prioritisation, implementation, and monitoring of programmes. Given the Indian psyche to expect everything from the government community participation requires active persuasion. In an urban environment, it is seen as next to impossible. Public tolerance is very high which results in poor public response. For promoting and developing people's participation the Ninth five-year plan (1997-2002) called for creating effective institutions for a participatory planning process. The facilitators need to come from all occupations such as political leaders, social activists, philanthropists, corporate managers, and government agencies. There is evidence that voluntary organisations, co-operatives, corporate sector and government agencies have designed and implemented successful development programmes through people's participation. An example is the development plan in Kerala, which was steered by the People's Plan Campaign (PPC) through the three-tier Panchayat system. The essential components of institutional reform that have been identified are: assessment of local resources and local level planning, sensitising people and building local organisations for collective actions and an umbrella support mechanism to facilitate people's development actions. If this process and mechanism has to be multiplied on a national scale, it has to be institutionalised. According to the Planning Commission, this requires a major political commitment to create the political space and policy framework for a sensitive support mechanism.

# 4

# An Envisioned Future:
## Reshaping India's National Maritime Vision

*I dream of an India which is counted among the ranks of developed nations before the end of the second decade in the new century.*

**Atal Behari Vajpayee**

*If there is one place on the face of earth where all the dreams of living men have found a home from the very earliest days when man began the dream of existence, it is India.*

**Romain Rolland**

*So far as I am able to judge, nothing has been left undone, either by man or nature, to make India the most extraordinary country that the sun visits on his rounds. Nothing seems to have been forgotten, nothing overlooked.*

**Mark Twain**

A nation's outward character is influenced by its geo-political location, historical experience and economic strength. Geo-politically, India's Ocean domain, which nearly equals its landmass, lies right across the busiest highways in the world. Centuries before history was ever recorded in 3000 BC, India and Babylon were engaged in maritime trade. Economically, India, one of the bronze age civilisations, symbolised by populous cities, highly skilled industries, far-flung commerce and a pictographic script was a country of wealth and prosperity.

India is a nation with a decisive maritime character with its vast ocean domain, far-reaching dependence on maritime access for economic well-being and a rich maritime history. Despite its inherent maritime character, India has never fully embraced its maritime dimension, often to its own detriment. A land-centric national strategy, and with 3/4$^{th}$ of the one billion population living away from the coast, makes it fundamentally difficult for Indians to understand the importance of maritime access for economic, political and military purposes. And, unless India develops a sense of confidence and ideology regarding its maritime character, the contemporary crisis of inertia in affairs maritime will continue.

Today, almost every Indian depends on the ocean more than at any other time in our history, either, as source of food and raw materials or as a vital link for transport and trade. Further, the sea is a favoured destination for our leisure time and the location of our most valuable habitats and landscapes. The rapid political, technological, and social changes have intertwined the economics, environment and security of maritime resources creating a complex management situation. The underlying management problems relate to lack of knowledge, inappropriate and uncoordinated laws, failure to involve stakeholders and a lack of co-ordination between the relevant national, state and local administrative bodies. There is no simple legislative solution to these complex problems. Uncoordinated sectoral policies tend to conflict and at times even work at cross-purposes, resulting in policy gridlock. The diversity of physical, economic, cultural and institutional conditions makes it critical to find ways of improving convergence within the planning system between the different sectors.

To overcome some very serious challenges to national well being India needs a unified national maritime policy to provide a road map for the various uses of the ocean. The formulation of this unified national maritime policy is a government responsibility that comes from a blend of international and national laws as well as the nation's maritime strategy. Thus, maritime affairs have a complex political dimension. Broadly, India is interested in the use of the ocean for three purposes, namely, passage of trade and exploitation of ocean resources, protecting the marine ecosystem from environmental damage, and safeguarding the sovereign and territorial integrity of the nation. These are the underlying considerations in the whole business of Integrated Management of maritime affairs that can be conceived as a trinity, the idea of three in one.

The character of the trinity is defined by the three characteristic areas of policy action by which India needs to carry out its purposes: economic development, environmental protection and maritime security policies. Each of these policy areas serves a large variety of subordinate functions. The 'trinity of ocean policy spheres' are the building blocks of a unified national maritime policy that aims to provide consistency, coordination, coherence and compliance between strategies across sectors and levels of governance for good stewardship of the oceans. This entails identification of an agreed vision, objectives and action plan, balancing the concerns and interests of the multiple stakeholders and coordinating implementation of strategy action programmes.

The oneness of the trinity is provided by the idea of the use of the ocean for national interests. National interest contains the attributes of *inclusiveness*; that is it concerns the country as a whole or at least a sufficiently substantial subset to transcend the specific interest of particular groups, and *exclusiveness,* that is it need not necessarily include the interests of groups outside the state, although it may do so. The rules for its identification are given by the tenets of the political process that have an independent normative value - those of democratic procedure. National interest can best be identified when it resolves itself into a verifiable expression of national preferences (Griffiths et.al., 2002). It could be said that India's maritime national interests include anything that affects people's health [environment protection], economic well being [resource development and growth - energy, trade, commerce, living and non-living resources], social stability [intersociety and intergenerational equity] and political peace [maritime sovereignty and good order at sea].

The implementation of any unified national maritime policy in pursuance of India's maritime national interests, and the enforcement of rules and regulation requires interaction between the government and industry or the public and private sectors or the regulators and users or those seen to provide livelihood and those whose livelihoods depend upon the oceans. Whichever way one looks at it, balancing of sectoral and stakeholder interests is necessary to meet all the requirements of good stewardship of the oceans. Hence, good stewardship is about efficient and harmonious functioning of all aspects of ocean use. India is yet to attain this form of integrated management in maritime affairs.

## Economic Development Policy

India with four per cent of world trade share and 16 per cent of the world population in effect generates one per cent of world trade for every four per cent of the Indian population. Compare this to the world average of one per cent trade for 0.9 per cent of the world population and the enormity of the potential for economic growth stares in the face. In yet another comparison, India's share in world exports equals 0.7 per cent as compared to 77.1 per cent of the advanced economies with just 15.7 per cent of the world population. It brings new and emerging opportunities for maritime industries and ocean related coastal development. Collaboration, cooperation and coordination are needed to support and promote business development and make the maritime industry more competitive - to begin with shipping and ports, oil and gas, fisheries, and tourism sectors.

## Shipping and Ports

As India enters a period of sustained economic growth it has the potential to emerge as major market for container trade and provide a further stimulus to global container volumes. A United Nations Economic and Social Commission for Asia and the Pacific (UNESCAP) Study indicated that even as general cargo in developed countries has been 70-80 per cent containerised, the figure for India hovers around 50 per cent. India is expected to experience a 9.4 per cent increase rate of port container throughput from 2, 186 thousand TEU (Twenty Foot Equivalent Unit - containers) in 1999 to 6,140 thousand TEU in 2011. Ironically, despite this almost 80 per cent of Colombo's trans-shipment business of 4 million TEU in 2011 is expected to either originate in, or be destined for, an Indian destination. This corresponds to a 50 per cent share of the total Indian container market.

The potential for containerisation in India is vast. A world class container transhipment port is proposed to be developed at Vallarpadam in Kochi. In addition, Jawaharlal Nehru Port (JNP), Tuticorin and Chennai Port are proposed to be developed as hub ports. For Vallarpadam, JNP, Tuticorin and Chennai to become world class container ports will depend upon port performance and productivity. In 2002-03, the Average Pre Berthing Detention Time (APDT) at 1.13 days, the Average Turn Around Time (ATR) at 2.66 days, and the Average Output Per Ship Per Berth (AOSB) at 8506 tonnes was the best performance by the country's major ports in over a decade. Even this improved performance continues to be lower than the generally accepted international standards and performance of regional ports. The port tariffs levied based on the cost-plus approach are higher than neighbouring ports in the region It is an inappropriate pricing mechanism as it does not take into consideration the improvement in productivity and efficiency. To emulate the success of other container ports in the region such as Colombo, Dubai, Singapore, Hong Kong and Shanghai will therefore depend upon the ability to deliver a very high level of performance at a modest cost.

Indian shipping, with 17 per cent share in the carriage of overseas trade in 2002, is inadequate to support the country's projected trade volumes over the next decade. Even more dismissal is the share of Indian shipping in the carriage of container cargo, which is less than 5 per cent with Indian shipping companies operating only 10 cellular container vessels. As a result, India's imports are costlier and exports less competitive. This is basically due to longer transit time and additional port cost and results in the increased loss of foreign exchange on payment of freight to foreign ships. The growth of Indian shipping depends not only on a supportive fiscal policy including a competitive tax regime, but also a strong cargo support policy for the national tonnage.

In August 2003, the Government launched the 'Sagar Mala' project for rapid capacity expansion and modernisation of ports along India's west and east coasts. The aim is to enhance capacity, efficiency and connectivity at ports, boost shipping tonnage under Indian flags, increase the share of inland waterways, and promote coastal shipping. For this, the government proposes to set aside Rs 55,000 crore (Rs 550 billion) for the ports sector, Rs 25,000 crore (Rs 250 billion) for the shipping sector and Rs 26,000 crore (Rs 260 billion) for inland water transport and coastal shipping. As a first step, integrated development of Nhava Sheva and Kochi ports, at a cost of Rs.7500 crore, was to begin by March 2004. The shipping ministry has proposed a maritime development cess of Rs 50 per tonne of cargo to finance the Rs 1,00,000-crore Sagar Mala project. The cess will be credited to the Consolidated Fund of India and administered by the finance ministry. The total cargo currently being handled by all the ports in the country (including major, minor and intermediate ports) is over 400 million tonnes and the proposed cess will therefore yield Rs 2,000 crore per annum.

The successful implementation of the 'Sagar Mala' project will depend upon the coordination between multiplicities of stakeholders in the maritime sector. It requires the formation of a permanent consultative committee at the Centre and each of the coastal states for coordination between the Centre and the States, ministries/departments of shipping, tourism, agriculture, environment, petroleum and natural gas, defence, home, finance, commerce, shipping companies, ports, railways, highways, inland waterways, customs and excise authorities, security agencies, and environmental bodies. This is to avoid bottlenecks and duplication or multiplication, or other inter-departmental hurdles in the implementation process of the programme.

## Oil and Gas

India has very high energy import dependence. India imports 70 per cent of its crude oil requirement. The Government of India (GoI) is taking steps to enhance indigenous crude production to bridge the growing gap between indigenous production (currently 32 million tonnes) and likely demand which is expected to reach 244 million tonnes in 2011 and 370 million tonnes in 2020-21. The demand for oil and natural gas which together make up about 42 per cent of the energy requirement is likely to grow at the rate of 5.6 per cent per year in the case of oil. The growth in consumption of natural gas is expected to increase from the current level of 65 MMSCMD to 130 MMSCMD in 2006-07 and would approximately be 391 MMSCMD by 2025, indicating that dependency on natural gas would also increase in the future.

India has 26 sedimentary basins comprising both inland and offshore areas. The total sedimentary basin area of India is around 1.784 million sq km up to 200m isobath, of which 0.498 million sq km is moderate to well explored and 0.601 million sq km is unexplored. The total sedimentary area for deep waters is around 1.356 million sq km, most of which remains to be explored. Immense efforts in exploration have resulted in an estimated prognostic hydrocarbon resource base of about 29 billion tonnes of oil and equivalent gas, including 7 billion tons from deep offshore. Out of this, only 6.8 billion tonnes of geological reserve have been established through exploration. This leaves a substantial resource base unexplored. Of the total prognostic hydrocarbon resources of India, 33 per cent lie onshore, 42 per cent offshore (up to 200m water depth) and 25 per cent lie in deep waters. India's reserves of oil at the end of 1999 were about 600 million tonnes (a share of 0.5 per cent of world's oil reserves) and natural gas reserves were about 650 billion cubic metres (0.4 per cent of world's reserves). With sustained efforts towards petroleum exploration and exploitation, India has also ventured into new frontier areas like Coal Bed Methane(CBM), deep-water exploration (beyond 200m isobath) and gas hydrates.

India's demand for energy is great and growing. Energy security is the most critical economic component of maritime security. The import of oil from Gulf is vital to meeting our energy demand and involves limiting the vulnerability to oil supply disruptions. This is essentially a short-term issue. The long-term concern is the smooth functioning of the international energy system that guarantees supplies to meet the rising demand at reasonable prices. Given that India is a net importer of oil and certainly cannot be dependent on the international energy system, India could act proactively to adopt and implement strategies such as building oil stockpiles, investing in equity oil abroad and developing alternative sources of energy.

On 07 January 2004, the GoI announced its decision to set up strategic oil storage facilities at three locations on the East and West coasts at an estimated cost of Rs 1, 650 crore for the construction of the facilities; Rs 5,000 crore for 5 million tonnes of crude to be stored; and, Rs 29 crore towards annual maintenance costs. The strategic storage of oil would be enough to meet the countries requirement for 15 days. Amongst the various measures to tide over short term oil disruptions stock draw from stockpiles is probably the most effective means for restoring normalcy in the domestic oil market. A study commissioned by Asia Pacific Energy Research Centre (APERC) in 2002 concluded that given the high costs for financing and maintaining stockpiles, for smaller Asian oil importing economies, like Thailand a stockpile of around 30 days coverage of net imports would be optimal in terms of costs versus benefits. In the development of strategic storage joint stockpiling must also be considered as a viable option. For India, this can translate in two ways. Firstly, India could enter into a joint stockpiling scheme with SAARC members and secondly India could enter into a strategic partnership with Russia to further bolster its own stockpile. A spot stockpile at sea may be more cost effective and economically viable with greater return on investment by maintaining a fleet of VLCCs at sea. As per current market estimates cost of a single VLCC can be recovered in one to one and a half years in its optimal life span of 25 years.

## Alternative Energy Resource

As for alternative sources of energy some of the options include tidal, thermal and wind production of energy. Technological advances in these fields are yet to fully develop to provide viable forms of alternative sources of energy. The potential sites for tidal energy include the Gulf of Cambay, the Gulf of Kachchh on the west coast and the Ganges Delta in the Sunderbans on the East Coast. The identified economic tidal power potential in India is of the order of 8000-9000 MW. The Gulf of Cambay has a potential of about 7000 MW where the average tidal range is 6.77 m (maximum 11 m). The Gulf of Kachchh with an average tidal range of 5.23 m (maximum 8 m) has a potential of about 1200 MW. The Sunderbans with an average tidal range of 2.97 m (maximum 5 m) has a potential of less than 100 MW. The Kachchh Tidal Power Project with an installed capacity of about 900 MW is estimated to cost about Rs. 1460.00 crore generating electricity at about 90 paise per unit. From the 201 wind stations as having potential for wind power generation as many as 186 wind stations are located in the coastal States/ UTs. The estimated wind power potential considering only one per cent of land availability is around 34842 MW (Table 4.1). The Ocean Thermal Energy Conversion (OTEC) cell at the Indian Institute of Technology and the National Institute of Ocean Technology both located in Chennai are involved in Research and Development (R&D) projects in OTEC. The world's first floating OTEC power plant of one-megawatt capacity is near completion near Tuticorin.

It may also be stated that in recent year's natural gas has emerged as an environmentally friendly alternative for oil. Then there is the option of international gas pipelines. Given the politics connected with gas pipeline projects, India will see LNG based natural gas imports before pipeline based gas. Dahej in Gujurat (Petronet) received its first LNG consignment on 09 February 2004 and Shell's venture at Hazira is nearing completion. India could be the final destination for 3 major transnational gas pipelines from Iran, Turkmenistan and Bangladesh. However, smooth and continuous supplies depend on multi-country agreements. Such international agreements may not always be possible.

## Fisheries

The fisheries sector is the predominant maritime sector in the socio-economic development of the country. More than six million fishermen and fish farmers across 3937 coastal villages besides fishing hamlets and reservoirs, depend on fisheries and aquaculture for their livelihood. India is the third largest fish producer in the world and second in inland fish production. The fisheries sector contributes Rs 19,555 crore to the national income which is 1.4 per cent of the total GDP and is a major contributor the foreign exchange earnings of the country through exports.

**Table 4.1: Wind Power Potential in Coastal States/UTs**

| S. No. | Coastal State/ Union Territory | Stations with annual Avg. WPD > 200 W/m$^2$ at 50m height as on 31 Dec. 2002 | Gross Potential (Mega Watts) |
|---|---|---|---|
| 1 | Andaman and Nicobar Islands | 01 | NA |
| 2 | Lakshadweep Islands | 08 | NA |
| 3 | Gujarat | 34 | 7362 |
| 4 | Maharashtra | 25 | 4519 |
| 5 | Karnataka | 26 | 7161 |
| 6 | Kerala | 16 | 1026 |
| 7 | West Bengal | 01 | 32 |
| 8 | Orissa | 06 | 1520 |
| 9 | Andhra Pradesh | 29 | 9063 |
| 10 | Tamil Nadu | 40 | 4159 |
| 11 | Total | 186 | 34842 |

*Source:* Centre for Wind Energy Technology (www.cwet.tn.nic.in)

During the last five decades, fish production has increased with an annual growth rate of 4.1 per cent. Marine capture fisheries play a vital role in the Indian economy. The sector provides employment and income to nearly two million people. Marine fish production level has risen from 0.52 mt in 1950-51 to 2.81 mt in 2002-03 with a growth rate of 3.43 per cent. However, most of the major commercially exploited stocks are showing signs of over exploitation. With the growing demand for seafood the country needs to formulate and adopt a new deep sea fishing policy for sustainable development of the fisheries resources in the Exclusive Economic Zone. A deep sea fishing policy consistent with national interests would address the impact on near-shore fisheries. Apprehensions of negative impact on near-shore fisheries coupled with the present gap in the potential and current exploitation has numerous economic repercussions from the land-locked states (Nepal and Bhutan) staking a claim to illegal poaching by foreign fishing vessels. In effect our fisheries resource base in the EEZ would be exploited for the benefit of third parties. India also needs to adopt measures for exploiting fisheries resources on the High Seas to be able to stake a claim to the resource alongside other countries. To be internationally competitive in the exports of marine products the existing fishing harbours and associated infrastructure needs modernisation for a high fish quality assurance. The tenth plan has proposed a fish production target of 8.19 mt envisaging an aggregate growth rate of 5.44 per cent (marine growth rate of 2.5 per cent and inland growth rate of 8.0 per cent). The main thrust for fisheries development is to concurrently utilise the full potential of inland and deep sea fisheries to substantially increase the per capita consumption of fish from the present level of nine kg per head per annum.

## Tourism

Both, the West and East Coast of India offer unparallel variety of sun, surf and sand - placid lagoons and backwaters, marine estuaries teeming with fish, bays and rough lava-rocked seas, the crashing surf, pure powdery golden sand or palm fringed shores - that cannot be found anywhere else in the world. Added to this natural beauty, nine of the 18 world heritage cultural sites in India are along the Indian coastline (Appendix 4). The pristine coastline has the potential to transform India into one of the most favoured tourist destinations in the world. Recognising the interdependence and indivisibility of economic development, environment protection and maritime security policy spheres is central to the attainment of this far-reaching goal.

## Environment Protection Policy

For a better world to live in, the quality of life is intrinsically dependent on the quality of air we breathe, the water we use, the greenness of our environment and the richness of our biodiversity. Marine biodiversity merits six of the seventeen world heritage sites located in India, fourteen biosphere reserves, six Ramsar wetlands, and is one of the twelve global centres of origin of cultivated plants. In total about 3.16 million km2 (or 4.4 per cent) of the land area is protected for its nature conservation value. India, with 2.4per cent of the world's hot spot area, has 8.1per cent of the world's total biodiversity with one of the two hotspots the Western Ghats on the West Coast. The aquatic ecosystem of the country supports 30 per cent of the world's flora and 6.67 per cent of world's animal species.

India's legislative framework for environment protection is more or less in line with developed nations and is also signatory to the major international conventions. Central and State Pollution Control Boards have been set up for their implementation. The Environment Protection Act, 1986, National Water Pollution Act, 1987 and Coastal Regulation Zone notification issued in 1991, principally regulate the marine environment. Yet, there is evidence that environmental degradation continues. A look at the water quality monitoring results indicates that organic and bacterial contamination continues to increase, affecting the health of the Indian aquatic resources. Outstanding natural features as well as important flora and fauna habitats should be afforded strict conservation status. The maintenance and enhancement of natural processes can increase the resilience of the coastline against coastal erosion and accelerated sea level rise. Mitigation of adverse effects of developments that cannot be avoided, by restoration of the habitat is a compensatory mechanism that is to be used as a last resort. There is, therefore, a definite need to reduce the gap between environment protection concept and practice along our coastline.

Coastal States are seeking a reversal of the present laws regulating the coastline and empowerment of Coastal States to pass their own laws. At the same time the Government after two failed attempts in 1991 and 1994 is attempting to move towards a comprehensive environment policy. Clearly, there a difference in perceptions on environment protection that also indicates that a regulatory framework by itself is not sufficient for sustainable development. The economic and ecological interests of the different stakeholders create conflict between development and environment in terms of short-term private economic interests and long-term public interest of sustainable resource use (Visser, 1999). It is increasingly necessary for the government to develop private-public partnerships to fully accomplish the goals of their development initiatives related to the maritime zone. Effective conflict resolution requires a conception of public policy making in which all stakeholders have an opportunity to negotiate.

A failure in knowledge diffusion is one of the key reasons for continuing destruction of coastal landscapes, seascapes and resources. Many of the problems of the maritime zone can be traced to the fact that the required information or understanding has never reached the correct audience. The diffusion of information, knowledge and understanding of the natural processes can help planners, decision makers and the general public to realise the consequences of any particular action, and provide the basis for developing more sustainable policy and management actions in the maritime zone. An informed public will allow two-way communications among government agencies, users groups, and local communities to ensure the social acceptability necessary to enhance the successful implementation and enforcement of decisions for sustainable development. This will require empowering our Panchayati Raj Institutions (local level) to take decisions essential to achieving the objectives of environment protection - quality of life, cultural and social heritage, rich biodiversity and leisure time pursuits.

There is thus a need for a better understanding of the interactions and interdependencies of sustainable development. To overcome the procedural, planning, policy and institutional weaknesses requires a formalised systematic and comprehensive Strategic Impact Assessment (SIA) to take account of the cumulative impacts of a development. This will allow promulgating non-development zones and protected areas with a view to control the scale of activities in relation to the natural, cultural and physical characteristics of the surrounding area. It will enable the preservation of the local cultural heritage by relocating development not dependent on the maritime zone, phasing out ongoing harmful activities and reserving potential development sites for future developments.

The management options must be based on the precautionary principle. Using Hey's definition the principle dictates that comprehensive methods of environmental, social, cultural and economic assessment must be used in deciding upon measures to enhance the quality of the coastal and marine area (McIntyre and Mosedale, 1997). Environment protection decisions as far as possible need to be made on the basis of the best available information adopting economically, environmentally and socially sound measures that act as incentives for the conservation and sustainable use of the maritime zone. Finally, part costs of measures to prevent, control, and reduce damage to the biological diversity and coastal landscapes and seascapes need to be borne by the user.

## Maritime Security Policy

India's maritime security concerns have to look far beyond any immediate threats in the neighbourhood and develop increasingly according to the requirements of a resurgent nation, The world ratio of 2:1 of ocean space to land space is indicative of the area available for exploitation for communications, including underwater fibre optic cables and pipelines, raw materials, food as well as a natural environment for human existence in the future. There is therefore a need to cease obsession with pure military dangers and concentrate upon measures to deal with very different challenges to national well being.

In an era of rapid economic growth, nations are attaching considerable importance to maritime issues such as, jurisdictions, trade routes, fishing rights, offshore resources, transit rights, piracy, drug trafficking and illegal immigration. This is significantly influencing every nation's perception of the regional environment in relation to their maritime power. Today, India's maritime potential lies in its economic capacity, democratic values, rich cultural heritage, desire for just, fair and equitable relations between all nations and most significantly its strategic geographic location in the Indian Ocean.

India's maritime zone that extends beyond the visible coastline and depicted by imaginary lines at sea requires safeguarding our national interests across an ocean space nearly equal to the whole of India. Added to that as the economic strength of the nation grows, it is giving rise to increased concerns of economic, environmental and resource security and fundamentally entails safeguarding our national interests against sea borne threats. This broadening of concept has come about as a result of the recognition that non-military threats are as important as military threats. Maritime security is linked to economic development and environmental protection in a number of ways.

Economically, besides the fact that 90 per cent of our trade by volume and 77 per cent by value moves over the seas, the security of our living ocean resources and the assurance of a safe and secure environment for tourists are key determinants of the maritime security paradigm. In addition, whatever be the source of energy, India will continue to be dependent on the transportation of energy, over the sea or land requiring considerable investment in naval capabilities for protection of our Sea Lines of Communication and a variety of naval, ground and air assets to guard any future oil or gas pipelines.

Environmental degradation anticipates actual or possible conflict between and within nation's over scarce resources, including water and arable land, and the environmental services they provide. The security paradigm focuses concern on increased social tensions and political instabilities within states as a result of environmental degradation and the inequitable distribution of resources and disproportionate vulnerabilities to environmental change. This fits with a more traditional security paradigm, even if the threats are defined as non-military in nature.

Finally, resource security is concerned with crime at sea arising from issues of piracy, terrorism and insurgency, drug trafficking, illegal arms trade and even marine safety. Safeguarding areas abundant in natural resources from illegal exploitation and security of the maritime infrastructure such as ports and offshore infrastructure are some of the additional resource security concerns.

While India enjoys sovereign rights for managing and conserving resources in the Exclusive Economic Zone there is conflict of interests in the application of the principle of 'Freedom of the Seas' with some of the major maritime powers. The UK, France and US continue to use the principle to further military intelligence gathering. Finally, outstanding boundary demarcation issues with Pakistan and Bangladesh impinge on the maritime sovereignty rights of the nation. These are non-traditional military dangers that require an appropriate diplomatic and operational response capability.

Effectively, the Integrated Management strategy in the context of maritime security puts forward that (i) India has interests and obligations in maritime activities occurring within its maritime zone; (ii) India requires a range of potential responses - diplomatic, operational, political, legal and non-governmental - to manage the multiple activities; and (iii) India must maintain or have access to capabilities for surveillance, monitoring and control.

The maritime zone surveillance, monitoring and control challenge requires a well coordinated military and police interface. Based on a classification by Geoffery Till, amongst the 159 nations listed in the 2003 *Jane's Fighting Ships*, 65 nations can be said to be operating a navy that are ranked between an inshore territorial defence navy and a major global force projection navy (Table 4.2). The balance 94 nations have a constabulary/ token navy of which 62 nations maintain only patrol forces, while 12 nations have patrol forces and a Coast Guard/ equivalent force and the remaining 20 nations have only a Coast Guard/equivalent force.

Between the US and Russia - the two global force projection navies - there is a striking contrast in the approach to dealing with maritime threats in the geographic areas under their national jurisdictions. The US Coast Guard maintains a national defense role under the new Department of Homeland Security. 13 US Navy corvettes are placed under the tactical control of the US Coast Guard while remaining under the operational control of the US Navy. On the other hand, Russia, which maintains a Federal Border Service under the Ministry of Interior, identifies the Russian Navy's immediate task until 2007 to be in a position to safeguard Russian sovereign interests and ensure security in all adjacent sea areas, even as the Russian Navy proceeds to re-establish its presence in the Indian Ocean in the foreseeable future.

Interestingly, some of the other principal nations -UK, France, Germany, Italy, Spain, Japan, Canada and Australia - are governed by different defence pacts in which US is a key partner. In the case of Japan and Australia, maritime surveillance is the domain function of the Japanese Maritime Self Defence Force (JMSDF) and Royal Australian Navy (RAN), respectively. In addition, the RAN patrol forces for the 21st century will be used to protect the EEZ, undertake search and rescue, and prevent illegal activities. China operates four regular para-military security forces in addition to the PLA Navy.

**Table 4.2: Nations Operating Naval and Other Constabulary Forces**

| | Only Naval forces | Constabulary force integral to the Navy | More than one constabulary force | Single Constabulary force | Constabulary force with defense role | Total |
|---|---|---|---|---|---|---|
| Major Global Force Projection Navy | | | | Russia | United States | 2 |
| Medium Global Force Projection Navy | | | United Kingdom, France, Germany, Italy, Spain | | | 5 |
| Medium Regional Force Projection Navy | Brazil | | China, Japan, India, | | | 4 |
| Adjacent Force Projection Navy | Israel, Portugal, South Africa, Libya, Iran, Romania, Colombia, Bulgaria, Yugoslavia, North Korea | | Canada, Australia | South Korea, Argentina, Algeria, Chile, Greece, Taiwan, Thailand, Turkey | | 20 |
| Offshore Territorial Defence Navy | Mexico, New Zealand, Nigeria, Syria, Uruguay | Norway, Denmark | Malaysia, Indonesia, Pakistan, Singapore | Sweden, Netherlands, Poland, Ukraine, Croatia, Ecuador, Egypt, Peru, Venezuela, Philippines | | 21 |
| Inshore Territorial Defence Navy | Bangladesh, Belgium, Myanmar, Vietnam | | Finland, Estonia, Lithuania, Morocco, Saudi Arabia, Bahrain, Oman, United Arab Emirates, Yemen | | | 13 |
| Total | 20 | 2 | 23 | 19 | 1 | 65 |

Note: Another 65 nations have constabulary navies and balance 20 of the 159 nations only have a Coast Guard/equivalent force.

Of the 65 nations (Table 4.2), 45 nations have a Navy and a role specific Coast Guard/equivalent force. The need for maintenance of border integrity vis-à-vis arms trafficking, illegal immigration, smuggling and crime at sea exists up to the contiguous zone (24 mm). It requires merging the assets of a multitude of agencies (charged with the responsibility), such as, customs, police, fisheries, environment into the Coast Guard or equivalent force to function as a unified maritime law enforcement agency. In addition, the Coast Guard or its equivalent force undertakes fisheries resource protection, environmental response and protection, and search and rescue. What is needed is a composite constabulary force to deal with the domestic responsibilities having implications on maritime security that include:-

a) Policing the waters up to the territorial sea (12 nm) including port security and waterways management.

b) Customs, fiscal, immigration and sanitary law enforcement up to the contiguous zone (24 nm).

c) Prevention of illegal fishing in the Exclusive Economic Zone (200 nm).

d) Responding to an environmental disaster and protecting the marine environment from pollution in the Exclusive Economic Zone (200 nm).

e) Safety of life and property at sea in the Search and Rescue Region (SRR).

The Navy responsible for maritime security – piracy, terrorism, weapon proliferation, Weapons of Mass Destruction, regional conflict, force projection – would need to undertake maritime patrol and surveillance for monitoring and control in the EEZ. The Navy and Coast Guard, configured as such, would allow optimisation of assets and provide a joint response capability to a wide range of threats, at varying levels of intensity across the full spectrum of maritime security concerns — military and constabulary.

## The National Maritime Vision

An examination of the trinity of policy spheres – economic development, environment protection, and maritime security – underscores the challenges we face and requires us to give up long held assumptions and practices to be replaced with new mind-sets and behaviour, while remaining true to our national interests. A national maritime policy with a view to safeguard national interests at all times will ensure that the management of maritime affairs is politically correct, environmentally sustainable, economically equitable, socially responsible and culturally sensitive. This requires articulation of a national maritime vision.

Building a (national maritime) vision is not about writing formal statements or establishing stretch goals. Rather, it is to do more with people (stakeholders) discovering who they truly are as an (integrated) organisation so that they can get on with the work of initiating growth and change (Stone, 1996). A well conceived vision is said to consist of two main components - core ideology and envisioned future (Collins et.al., 1996). The mastery of Collins and Poras in building visions is important in understanding these critical components, before any attempt is made in trying to articulate a national maritime vision. The core ideology defines, the enduring character of an organisation and consists of core values - system of guiding principles and tenets, and a core purpose - the organisation's most fundamental reason for existence. Core values are a small set of timeless guiding principles that have an intrinsic value and importance to those within the organisation. Core purpose is the organisation's reason for being and captures the soul of the organisation. The envisioned future consists of a 10 to 30 year audacious goal and a vivid description of what it will be like to achieve the goal. A vision level that describes Big Hairy Audacious Goals (BHAGs - pronounced BEE hags) serves as a unifying focal point of effort and acts as a catalyst for team spirit. It has a clear finish line; so that organisations know when it has been achieved. It is tangible, energising and highly focussed. Setting the BHAGs requires thinking beyond the current capabilities and the current environment. In addition to BHAGs, an envisioned future needs a vivid description that is vibrant, engaging and specific description of what it will be like to achieve BHAGs.

The maritime national interests are concerned with the people's health, economic well being, social stability and political peace. In keeping with our national interests, the core values of the national maritime vision could be stated as:-

(a) Protecting the marine environment.

(b) Economic resource development and growth.

(c) Intersociety and intergenerational equity.

(d) Maritime sovereignty and good order at sea.

The core values help in identifying the core purpose of integrated management of maritime affairs, which, it emerges, is to do with delivering ocean governance. The "ocean circle" adapted by Elisabeth Mann Borgese from Gandhi's *India of My Dreams*, is a United Nations agenda for ocean governance.

In this structure, composed of innumerable villages,
There will be ever-widening, never ascending circles.
Life will not be a pyramid
With the apex sustained by the bottom.
***But it will be an ocean circle,***
Whose centre will be the individual,
Always ready to perish for the village,
The latter ready to perish for the circle of villages
***Till at last the whole becomes one life,***
Composed of individuals.
Never aggressive in their arrogance, but ever humble,
***Sharing the majesty of the ocean circle,***
***Of which they are integral units.***
Therefore, the outermost circumferences
Will not wield power to crush the inner circle,
But will give strength to all within,
***And will derive its own strength from it.***

—*Mahatma Gandhi*

In the context of the core values of the national maritime vision, it means that India is an ocean circle, where the whole becomes one life composed of individual maritime sectors, sharing the majesty of the ocean circle of which they are integral units, giving strength to all within, and deriving their own strength from it. The core purpose of the national maritime vision could now be stated as - *to provide good governance and to be a role model for ocean governance.*

Prior to defining a 10 to 30 year audacious goal, it is significant to recount the Indian dream, which is to be counted in the ranks of developed nations by the end of the second decade of the century. This emphasises the need for a goal for maritime India that is tangible, energising, highly focussed, serves as a unified focal point of effort and acts as a catalyst for team spirit with a clear finish line. Using the core values and the core purpose in consonance with the Indian dream, a 10 to 30 year goal could be stated as - *becoming the fastest growing developed nation and transforming the developed maritime sector into one of the most sustainable in the world, by 2025.*

All that now remains is to translate the vision from words into pictures with a vivid description that is vibrating, engaging and specific in describing what it will be like to achieve the BHAG. Passion, emotion and conviction are essential parts of this vivid description (Collins *et.al.,* 1996). A vivid description of India's maritime vision, so to speak is that - *we will create a port and waterways infrastructure, together with the inter-modal connections that is globally competitive, as one of the most dependable all-weather transportation system for moving goods and people, supporting our omnipresent shipping in carrying our trade and Indian flagged vessels will be as well known as any other flagged vessel in the world. Our ship building programme will rival the most competitive shipyards anywhere. India will be self-reliant in energy, appraising the total prospects of our outer continental shelf to increase our indigenous production of oil and obtaining equity share of energy in other sedimentary basins around the world besides realising the full potential of our alternative sources of energy - natural gas, coal bed methane, tidal, wind, and thermal. India will be the first country in the world to undertake commercial deep-sea mining of manganese nodules and other minerals. Our tourist destinations, will signify the rich biodiversity of our marine ecosystem and our ocean heritage, and the quality of water at our beaches will be the safest and cleanest anyone can find anywhere on this planet. Our healthy bountiful living ocean resources, will be a productive source of food and medicine for all generations and our seafood will be the most sought after in the world market. Our understanding of the power of the oceans, disaster preparedness and coast protection measures for protecting human life and property, together with sustainable economic practices, will free our coasts from the catastrophic effects of man-made and natural disasters and our coastal communities will enjoy a quality of life unparalleled anywhere. Our interdisciplinary oceanographic and Antarctica research programmes, coupled with cutting-edge technology, will heighten our people's awareness of the ocean issues, strengthen our maritime power and inspire our scientists to study the oceans, in its oneness for the benefit of all mankind. Our Exclusive Economic Zone will epitomise safe and secure seas and international shipping will enjoy the ensuing safe navigation and the freedom of the seas. Our sea power and the work with other nations together will shape the Indian Ocean environment as a zone of peace and stability, for the destiny of the world to be decided on its waters. Our People joining hands and coming together will be our strength in the realisations of our maritime vision and living in India will mean something which is just out of this world - simply heaven on earth.*

For India to commit to this national maritime vision of the future requires answers to four components of the governance framework, which will move us from sectoral to participative management. The first priority would be to create a representative framework that has the mandate to take a wide-ranging perspective in formulating and coordinating a national maritime policy in pursuance of the nation's stated maritime vision. Second, the policy should be firmly synthesised into the national three tier governance architecture, recognising that co-operation can generally promote confidence building and enhance national development. Management of maritime affairs is not effective if all levels of administration do not support it, especially all the relevant sectoral branches of administration concerned with the maritime zone. Third, the policy implementation initiatives must be rooted in a thorough understanding of the local circumstances. Diverse conditions in the physical, social, cultural, economic and institutional characteristics of the area require adopting a site-specific context. This allows an appreciation of the pressures and driving forces that are influencing the dynamics of the local area. Finally, there must be recognition of the role of civil society as it works to build the opinions and perspectives of all relevant stakeholders into the planning process through collaborative involvement, reducing conflict and developing consensus.

# 5

# Organisational Structure:
## A Winning Model for India's Maritime Affairs

*What we need today, perhaps, is not a new theory, concept or framework but people who think strategically.*

**Kenichi Ohmae**

The previous chapter put forward a new thinking on an envisioned future of affairs maritime. Having situated an envisioned future, and put together the IM concept for achieving the stated objectives we come to the challenge of implementation and deliverance. The real need is to integrate every aspect of maritime affairs - political, economic, financial, technological, environmental, legal, and security - into the strategy implementation effort to turn vision into reality. The emergence of this new management paradigm forms the basis for the management of maritime affairs.

This entails a fundamental change in strategic thinking about how to implement policies at the national, state and local levels. What this essentially means is teamwork, because no one person, ministry or department, possesses all the information needed for decision making or has the expertise to implement policy decisions and monitor outcomes. There is no better way of managing maritime affairs than planning together and this requires developing a strategic framework.

A strategic framework provides for such a composite team and pooling resources to effectuate a common vision. It proffers some degree of institutionalised order and evidence of genuine commitment on part of all stakeholders.

To create alignment for preserving the core values and the core purpose while stimulating progress towards an envisioned future the strategic framework relies on political leadership (new direction), administrative processes (creative collaboration), and governance structures (new paradigm). Leadership is about providing morale and strategic vision to encourage a sense of direction and approach to shaping the future (Chowdhury, 2000). In the complex and dynamic marine environment governance without a shared agenda is like taking a ship out to sea without a compass. The concepts and tools of administrative processes that dominate our thinking about managing power, responsibility, authority, structure, hierarchy, control and coordination, needs to be re-examined for a truly creative collaboration of people committed to beating the odds. The process involves the breaking down of traditional boundaries to create horizontal networks that cut across all levels of governance (Chowdhury, 2000). Such internal networking creates a permeable, flexible and coordinated ocean governance structure that provides a new paradigm for managing the interdependent and indivisible maritime sector. This new paradigm for ocean governance is vital to connecting predisposed but isolated sectors and stakeholders to the core values and the core purpose of India's maritime vision. Without the internal networking it will be difficult to sustain significant change necessary to achieve the envisioned future of maritime India.

Essentially, management in the functional ministries and departments of this complex and dynamic marine environment have developed a high degree of differentiation in thought and pattern. To be effective in the complex and dynamic marine environment, the concerned ministries and departments need to develop the required state of inter-departmental integration. The ministry or department must function in unique ways to fulfill their individual purposes and must also coordinate to be completely effective in the realisation of India's maritime vision. It is important to understand that an organisation is not an independent entity, but rather an independent system - a result of complex interaction between itself and the environment (Hampton, 1979). A consistent organisation style may thrive in a highly competitive, undifferentiated and stable environment but is no virtue if it prevents the ministries and departments from coping effectively with the challenges and opportunities in a complex and dynamic (marine) environment.

## Conceptualising Governance

According to the Planning Commission, governance relates to the management of all such processes that in any society define the environment. Some of the approaches to conceptualising governance advocated by international organisations is shown in Table 5.1. The features of good governance are the exercising of legitimate political power; formulation and implementation of policies and programmes that are equitable; transparent, non-discriminatory, socially sensitive, participatory and, above all, accountable to the people at large. An independent assessment of governance in India has been undertaken by the United Nations Development Programme (UNDP) and in its Human Development Report 2001(Table 5.2).

**Table 5.1: Approaches to Conceptualising Governance**

## The World Bank

Governance is defined as the manner in which power is exercised in the management of a country's economic and social resources. The World Bank has identified three distinct aspects of governance (1) the form of political regime; (2) the process by which authority is exercised in the management of a country's economic and social resources for development; and (3) the capacity of governments to design, formulate and implement policies and discharge functions.

## United Nations Development Programme

Governance is viewed as the exercise of political, economic and administrative authority in the management of a country's affairs at all levels. It comprises mechanisms, processes and institutions through which citizens and groups articulate their interests, exercise their legal rights, meet their obligations, and mediate their differences.

## Organisation for Economic Cooperation and Development

The concept of governance denotes the use of political authority and exercise of control in a society in relation to the management of its resources for social and economic development. This broad definition encompasses the role of public authorities in establishing the environment in which economic operators function and in determining the distribution of benefits, as well as the nature of the relationship between the ruler and the ruled.

## Commission on Global Governance

Governance is the sum of the many ways individuals and institutions, public and private, manage their common affairs. It is a continuing process through which conflicting or diverse interests may be accommodated and cooperative action may be taken. It includes formal institutions and regimes empowered to enforce compliance, as well as informal arrangements that people and institutions either have agreed to or perceive to be in their interest.

**Table 5.2: India's Governance - Recent Report Card**

| Achievements | Concerns and Challenges |
|---|---|
| **Economic Governance** | |
| * India is among the ten fastest growing economies of 1990s;<br>* Substantial forward movement in industrial, trade and aspects of fiscal policy reforms;<br>*Tax reforms — rationalisation of tax rates, exemptions and simplification of tax<br>* Reasonable price stability;<br>* Comfortable balance of payments, growing foreign exchange reserves;<br>* Significant decline in incidence of poverty;<br>* Self-sufficiency in food grains with unprecedented public food stocks;<br>* Steady improvement in most social indicators;<br>* Impressive gains in demographic transition for many States. | * Growth disparities across States have increased in 1990s as compared to 1980s;<br>* Implementation problems remain in many areas and parallel action is needed in most States;<br>* Less than 0.5 per cent of population pays income tax, under reporting of income widespread;<br>* Stagnating tax — GDP ratio;<br>* Central and State Governments running unsustainable Fiscal Deficits;<br>* About 260 million persons or about 26 per cent of population still below the normative poverty line;<br>* Pockets of hunger and acute deprivation still an unfortunate reality;<br>* Critical gaps remain, a little less than half of women still illiterate, high infant mortality rates;<br>* Population growth still high, unsustainable and persisting adverse sex-ratios in some States. |
| **Politcal Governance** | |
| * A resilient democracy supporting the emergence of a multi-party polity at various tiers<br>* Politics of coalition and consensus is beginning to find its feet;<br>* Broad political consensus on nature and direction of economic reforms and national<br>* Movement on decentralisation of power from the Centre to States, districts and villages;<br>* Positive discrimination, reservation in political bodies at grass-root level, social mobilisation of the marginalised and competitive elections have created opportunities for popular participation in decision making;<br>* Independent and a proactive judiciary on issues of larger public interest. | * Absence of institutional framework for sustaining (coalition) governments for their term, once elected<br>* Recourse to competitive populism, the use of moneypower, particularly during elections, compromising decisive political action;<br>* Disruptions in parliamentary proceedings delaying timely and informed legislative work;<br>* Excessive compartmentalisation of the executive, into ministries resulting in a narrow development perspective, vested interests and preventing the rightsizing of a bloated bureaucracy;<br>* Criminalisation of public life, politics of vote bank, communal violence, and corruption are major challenges for improving governance in the country;<br>* Too much state presence in some areas, too little in others. |
| **Civil Governance** | |
| * Primacy of basic human and civic rights;<br>* Rule of law;<br>* Freedom of expression, free press and election<br>* Considerable non-governmental and civil society initiatives in various spheres of social<br>* Institutional framework/agencies for checking corruption in high public offices. | * Persisting law and order problems in some areas;<br>* Mobilisation of people for better work ethics, civic responsibilities and environmental protection;<br>* Poor conviction rates, delayed justice, backlog of cases, particularly in subordinate judiciary;<br>* Distorted, perverse incentive structures in civil services encouraging mediocrity and corruption.<br>* In practice, some like women and deprived are less equal than others, particularly, in their social and economic rights |

*Source*: National Human Development Report 2001

The following concerns and challenges are specially highlighted:-

a) Implementation problems remain in many areas and parallel action is needed in most States.

b) Excessive compartmentalisation of the executive, into ministries resulting in a narrow development perspective.

c) Mobilisation of people for better work ethics, civic responsibilities and environmental protection.

Having looked at the theoretical aspects of implementation and deiiverance of the national maritime vision, approaches to governance and an externally generated governance score card it becomes impetrative to look at current government thinking on governance for the tenth five-year plan (2002-2007) prior to suggesting a framework for realisation of India's maritime vision.

According to the tenth plan document, India cannot be content with just being one of the ten fastest growing economies in the world over the past two decades. The objective of the tenth five year plan is to make India the fastest growing country by end of 2007. In its preparation, the Planning Commission has not only involved the Central ministries and state governments, but has also involved academicians, subject experts, civil society organisations, trade unions and industrialists to take advantage of their expertise and ideas during the various stages of the plan preparation.

However, the successful implementation of development programmes requires adequate funds, appropriate policy framework and effective institutional capacity to deliver. The determining factor is the institutional capacity to formulate viable need based schemes or projects with efficient delivery systems to utilise optimally the available resources. Currently, there is insufficient convergence between the planning frameworks of different maritime sectors, both at the national and state levels; as also between these levels and between different sectors. As a consequence, multiple policies exist that are not synthesised by a common national vision for the maritime zone and, therefore, risk duplication, conflict, wastage of administrative and intellectual resources and greater financial costs. In its analysis of the functioning of the Central Government, the Planning Commission brings out that excessive compartmentalisation of the executive into ministries or departments has ensured that development programmes are not only spread over a host of ministries, which encourages a narrow sectoral approach to conceiving, formulating and implementing schemes, but also prevents mutual synergies to benefit the plan initiatives. There is duplication of delivery structures and procedural hurdles curtail translating the intended goals of development programmes into reality.

The tenth five year plan document, thus, reflects the need to address the first priority of reforming the institutional framework for management. In effect, good governance is perhaps the single most important factor in ensuring that India is the fastest growing economy by the end of 2007. Some of the key steps identified in the Tenth plan document that need to be undertaken on priority relate to:-

a) *Peoples Participation*: The involvement and participation of the people at all stages of planning, implementation and monitoring is a pre-requisite for good governance. People must feel a sense of ownership of the policy/plans/programmes/ projects and must participate and even contribute towards them. The trend of expecting the government to do everything for them must come to an end.

b) *Decentralisation*: The enactment of the 73rd and 74th Constitutional Amendment Bills, 1992 has paved the way for statutory institutional structures for realising the goals of self-governance, under the Panchayti Raj Institutions and urban local bodies. The explicit objective of this initiative for democratic decentralisation of governance is to accelerate the socio-economic development within a participatory framework at the grass-root level.

c) *Right to Information*: The right to information has to be the starting point for much of the proposed reforms. Very often people do not even know what the benefits of the proposed programmes/projects are and reforms can only be effective if people know what to expect from the overall policy/plan.

d) *Civil Society*: The role of civil society organisations as partners in the development of the nation lies in their inherent strengths of advocacy skills, organisational skills and being closer to the people.

e) *Programme/Project Formulation*: The programmes/ projects must have clear goals and objectives, strategies and action plans, a well defined delivery mechanism, establishing indicators for review and assessment and clearly identified responsibilities during the various stages of implementation.

f) *Synergy and Coordination*: The need for synergy and coordination between the different agencies engaged in the development programmes/projects is critical for obtaining the maximum benefit from limited resources, for minimising overheads, checking duplication of efforts and using resources and manpower optimally.

g) *Monitoring*: The absence of adequate monitoring and evaluation of the plan/ programmes/projects leads to considerable amount of wastage, leakages and spill over of schemes over successive five-year plans resulting in less than optimal use of scarce public resources in the development process.

So far, India has had a sectoral system of management. To highlight the point, the Planning Commission under the Ninth five-year plan had undertaken nearly 170 evaluation studies, and state evaluation organisations have completed 2200 evaluation studies of development schemes during the last forty years. From these reviews, it has emerged that programme implementation agencies have been created without the necessary associated institutional changes, leading to implementation by existing departments working independently for different components of a programme. In general, therefore, it can be argued that limitations in institutional capacities are the main barrier to improved planning and management of maritime affairs in the country.

A key question that remains is how to involve the Union, State, voluntary organisations, people, corporate sector, academics and scientists in a single management process? The conventional response to maritime affairs, based primarily on the production of new regulatory actions, has failed to reflect the complex and dynamic environment in which ministries and departments operate.

The Integrated Management (IM) of maritime affairs is meant to combine the ocean and coastal zone in a single unified framework, develop a shared vision amongst all the stakeholders and coordinates all the relevant policy areas, sectors and levels of administration in the short and long term. In general, the management process adopts the existing standard legal and administrative approaches, but the typical institutional framework differs from the line-agency (sectorally oriented) type of ministries and departments or the professional bureaucratic organisation. To qualify as 'integrated' there exists a need to find the right balance between national, state and local control in order to achieve a flexible collective that allows for creative collaboration in which a high degree of differentiation prevails as people with different skills, goals and time horizons work together.

The notion of collective captures the duality inherent in a creative process. A collective can be treated as singular when the collective is thought of as a whole (government) and as a plural when the individual members are thought of as acting separately (ministries and departments). Four conflicting paradoxes at the heart of the collective must be understood, accepted and as much as possible balanced (Chowdhury, 2000):-

a) Embracing individual differences, and collective identity and goals.

b) Fostering support and confrontation among members of the collective.

c) Focussing on performance and learning, and development.

d) Balancing the leader's authority, and the discretion and autonomy of the members of the collective.

The fundamental approach to such a collective is to adopt a strategy on innovative differentiation [Ostroff, 1999] that requires the resultant innovative organisation to:

a) Organise around cross-sectoral core processes, not individual activities.

b) Install process managers who will take responsibility for the core process in its entirety.

c) Make teams — not individuals — the cornerstone of organisational design and performance.

d) Decentralise power.

e) Integrate with the community.

f) Empower people by giving them the tools, skills, motivation and authority to make decisions essential to the team's performance.

g) Use information technology to help people reach the objectives of sustainable development.

h) Establish indicators to measure performance.

j) Undertake capacity building.

k) Develop a culture that focuses on continuous performance improvement through openness, co-ordination, co-operation and collaboration.

For any form of collective approach to work, the strategic framework has to be based on a co-ordinating mechanism at the highest level of government tasked to (Vallejo, 1993):

a) Generate information.

b) Carry out analytical studies for political decision-makers.

c) Reassess policies.

d) Undertake development of a long-term national maritime policy.

e) Strengthen multi-sectoral co-operation by improving linkages among sectors and administrative levels.

f) Provide overall guidance to the process of planning and implementation.

Clearly, the theoretical collective approach outlined and the key steps identified by the Planning Commission for good governance are similar. In the context of integrated management of maritime affairs, it implies that the strategic framework has more or less been identified by the government. The strategic framework only requires elucidation and formalisation at all levels of governance.

Essentially, the governance structure presently consists of political leadership (strategic apex), ministries/ departments at the national and state levels (administrative component), and the grass-root level Panchayti Raj institutions (operating core). The process of governance benefits from the contributions made by specialised people (advisory group) - scientists and academicians, voluntary organisations, environmentalists, economists, strategists, other subject experts and industrialists depending upon the specific issue under consideration.

Experts recommend a collaborative, co-operative and co-ordinated approach accommodated within the existing governmental framework. Thus, within the stated model of governance, the advisory group (plan preparation process for the Tenth five-year plan and the role of civil society) collates and provides information to the operating core (people's participation and decentralisation) for initial plan formulation. It then moves up to the administrative component for finalisation (programme/project formulation) with inputs from the advisory group and is given direction at the strategic apex. The strategic plan is then adopted, funded and put into operation by the national and state level administrative components. The operating core, assisted by the scientific institutions and voluntary organisations in the advisory group, undertakes continuous monitoring and evaluation to asses the impact of, and provide feedback for, corrective action to the administrative component. The resultant frequent and open vertical and horizontal communication would enable flow of information for all stakeholders to be aware of the developmental process. The strategic apex manages the entire process of strategy making. The framework achieves focus on the theme of integrated management through the mutual adjustment of all its actors (synergy and coordination). All that remains in developing the framework is a need to link the strategic apex, national and state level administrative components, operating core and the advisory group through a co-ordinating mechanism to avoid ambiguity, inefficiency and the resultant danger of an inappropriate transition that forces a return to the current system of governance. The co-ordinating mechanism with secretariat support will:

a) Avoid significant conflicts over major re-organisational initiatives (such as the creation of a new ministry).

b) Allow narrowly focussed sectoral planning to be broadened in scope by taking account of interactions and interdependencies.

c) Enable the involvement of all agencies and interest groups concerned with the maritime zone and its activities.

d) Help develop an overall focus with defined national interests.

e) Seek to develop both horizontal and vertical integration in planning, implementation, monitoring and evaluation.

f) Fulfil an organising, anchoring and supporting role by providing day to day coordination on a continuing basis within a broadly agreed time scale.

The secretariat support is needed for the following key tasks:-

a) Organising and coordinating the overall management process.

b) Gaining confidence and support of the administrative component, operating core and the specialised assemblage for the management process.

c) Planning specific activities meetings and events. Facilitating the setting of agendas at all stages of the management process and follow-up of decisions/ agreements.

d) Ensuring that roles of participants in the implementation processes are clearly established.

f) Acting as a communication focal point for information and enquiries.

g) Ensuring adherence to timetables.

The challenge lies in establishing a coordinating mechanism with secretariat support that commands the respect and trust of all the stakeholders and discharges its functions in an open and neutral way. International experience shows that the coordinating mechanism works best if it is located under the office of the President/Prime Minister or within a body that has the recognised authority for cross-sectoral coordination. When the coordinating mechanism is placed within a line ministry, there is danger that the management process will become, and be seen as, an activity of that ministry and will cease to command the wider acceptance and support that is needed. In the Indian context, at the national level, the Cabinet Secretariat or the Planning Commission are the recognised authorities for cross-sectoral coordination. Since the Planning Commission is concerned more with the plan formulation, the Cabinet Secretariat is more suited for the coordination of plan implementation. The Cabinet Secretariat support is however very limited and would need to be strengthened. At the level of states there is no similar body for cross-sectoral coordination.

Although, at the national level a coordinating mechanism could be constituted within the Cabinet Secretariat, for reasons of wider responsibilities of the Cabinet Secretariat and lack of adequate secretariat support it would be more efficient and effective to have an independent coordinating mechanism in the form of a coordination committee at the level of the Cabinet Secretary or the National Security Advisor who functions under the Prime Minister. The secretariat support for the coordination committee could easily be met from existing resources of the line ministries/ departments. A similar coordinating mechanism in the form of a Steering Committee needs to be set up in the coastal States/Union territories.

In summation, five distinct but interconnected institutional changes emerge from the current government thinking contained in the Tenth plan document and the theoretical framework. By an interpretation of the suggested framework, the following provides a reflection of the initiatives required:-

a) Formalising a 'Cabinet Committee for Oceans (CCO)' at the highest political level as the strategic apex that adopts the national maritime vision and provides leadership for integrated management of maritime affairs to make the transition from concept to practice.

b) Establishing a 'National Maritime Coordination Committee (NMCC)' with secretariat support as the 'Co-ordinating Mechanism' at the national level. The

NMCC assisted by the advisory group is authorised to formulate, monitor and evaluate the national maritime policy through a process of collaboration amongst all the concerned ministries and departments and different levels of government.

c) Creating a 'Maritime Steering Committee (MSC)' with secretariat support as the 'Co-ordinating Mechanism' at the level of coastal states/UTs. The MSC assisted by the advisory group should be authorised to steer plan/policy implementation between the state level administrative component and operating core and coordinate with the NMCC for monitoring and evaluation.

d) Empowering the 'Panchayti Raj Institutions (PRIs)' at the local level as the 'Operating Core'. The PRIs strengthened by the expertise available from the advisory group should be able to initiate plan formulation and after plan adoption by the administrative component be able to monitor and evaluate the development process.

e) Creating a 'Maritime Affairs Advisory Council (MAAC)' as the 'Advisory Group' to assist in the overall process of plan/policy/programme/project formulation, implementation, monitoring and evaluation. The MAAC is a network of specialised people to facilitate bringing of data together into a central repository that acts as a node for information dissemination and identification of gaps in knowledge. The MAAC is split into three divisions - national, state and local - with clearly defined functions of assisting national level plan/policy preparation, state level plan/policy/programme/project implementation and local level monitoring and evaluation to provide feedback to the national and state levels for corrective action.

The CCO provides vision through strategy-making and oversees the process of integrated management, administered through top-down policy formulation and adoption at the national level, and bottom up issue identification and implementation at the state level. The MAAC provides assessment and feedback for monitoring and evaluation by the PRIs and overall coordination by the NMCC and the MSC.

The framework requires no structural realignment of the current system of government; instead, it is absorbed within the existing administrative component of the government. There is no net loss of power or authority for any ministry or department. The strategic framework offers an opportunity to co-ordinate the planning, formulation, implementation, monitoring and evaluation necessary to achieve the overarching central government strategy for realisation of the national maritime vision.

# 6

# An Agenda for the 21$^{st}$ Century:

## Revitalising and Transforming Maritime Affairs

In understanding the maritime dimension it emerged that for the oceans there is no comprehensive strategy for tackling the interactions between trade, environment and security. The near absence of institutional mechanisms for coordination has resulted in ocean policy fragmentation, duplication of effort and wastage of financial resources. Consequently, the past two decades have witnessed unprecedented progress worldwide in attempting to formulate an ocean governance regime. The 1992 Rio conference through agenda 21, underlined the concept that management of maritime affairs must be integrated in content, precautionary in ambit and anticipatory in decision-making. Indeed the rapid political economic, technological, environmental, social and the recent security changes, post 11 September 2001 attacks on America, have created a complex management situation. For sustainable development of the maritime zone there is a change in emphasis from Freedom of the Seas to Control and Regulation in the management of maritime affairs.

The management of maritime affairs in national development requires a strategic approach, which is both long-term in its perspective and 'built-in' to the various development processes so that they are as complete as the challenges are complex. Formulating a strategic approach is about developing an underlying mission through consensual, effective and iterative process; and going on to set objectives, identify the means of achieving them and then monitor the achievements to be utilised as a guide in the next round of the learning process.

A strategic approach to maritime affairs at the national level implies:-

a) The need to consider the **Challenges** of the ocean space as a whole or 'Spatial Integration.'

b) **Coherence** between long term vision, medium term targets and short term action or 'Temporal Integration.'

c) Genuine **Collaboration** between government, industry, scientific and academic institutions, enforcement and regulatory agencies, non-governmental organisations and citizen groups since the management process is too complex to make do by any stakeholder acting alone or 'Stakeholder Integration.'

d) Inter-sectoral linkages so that there is a **Coordinated** approach to development or 'Sectoral Integration.'

e) Hierarchical linkages so that there is a **Convergence** in policy, development efforts and governance at Local, State, National and International levels or 'Institutional Integration.'

The five C's - Challenges, Coherence, Collaboration, Coordination and Convergence enables realisation of the five Ps - Plan, Ploy, Pattern, Position and Perspective in translating the integrated management concept to practice.

It can be argued that the integrated management of maritime affairs as derived earlier is a question of strategic management that broadly encompasses the areas of strategy formulation, implementation and control. In essence, the management process requires strategy evaluation from a holistic perspective and necessitates weighing interests and setting priorities at each level (Gupta and Fletcher, 2000). Having repositioned India as a maritime nation, reshaped the national maritime vision and put forward a winning model for the realisation of the maritime vision, what remains is to provide a road map for implementation.

The management of maritime affairs is about strategic intent to create value that meets the needs of all stakeholders across all maritime sectors. Not only does the management process facilitate fulfilling of social responsibilities, protecting the marine environment and safeguarding national interests but is also a prerequisite for sustainable development of the maritime zone. The focal point of the management process is creating economic wealth over the long term by holding advantage relative to competitive sectoral management.

According to Miller, the different forms of competitive advantage is differentiation, cost leadership and quick response (Figure 6.1). A successful differentiation strategy on the part of policy makers is to understand what the industry values, provide that value, and extracting a premium price for it from the industry. Cost leadership is a relative term that refers to costs relative to benefits and costs relative to competition. The cost leadership strategy would result in optimum utilisation of available resources, avoiding duplication of effort and overcoming high operational costs in planning and implementation as line department's work together. The resultant benefits of effective and efficient planning and implementation of projects when compared to competitive sectoral management would minimise costs of projects.

Figure 6.1: Competitive Advantage Strategies for IM

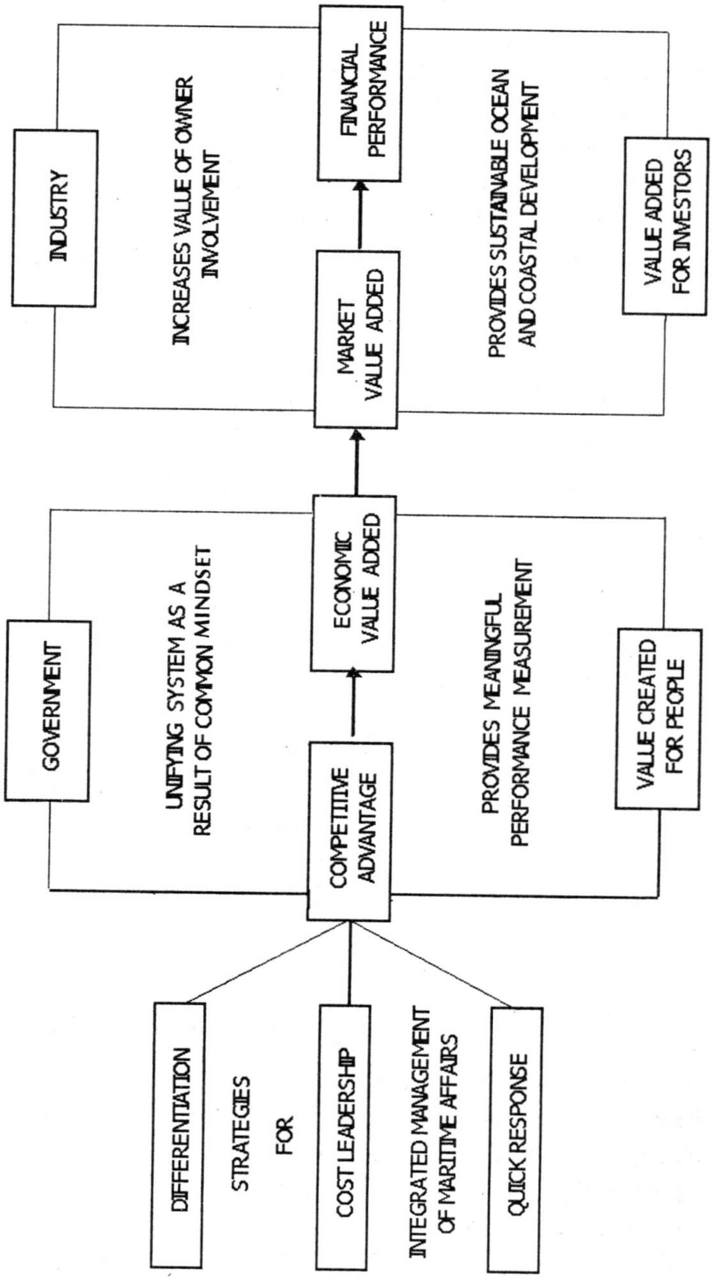

Quick response is a way of looking at the government's flexibility in dealing with the complex and dynamic marine environment. The management process provides competitive advantage as it allows the government to formulate, implement and monitor policies, plans, programmes and projects faster than under sectoral management.

A government that does not excel in any of the three sources of competitive advantage does not offer economic value to the people and will consequently fare normally. Normal performance is not noteworthy and there is no market value that is added. As a result, the financial performance of the industry as a whole yields normal profits which are just average and there is no real value added for the investors. Lack of economic value for the people and market value for investors has a direct impact on sustainability due to over-exploitation and disregard for environmental norms in an effort to enhance quality of life and increase return on investment. Thus, integrated management can be defined as the process of achieving tangible competitive advantage over sectoral management for sustainable development of the maritime zone.

Figure 6.2 lays out a systematic approach to strategy formulation, implementation and control. A top down approach or a national initiative to strategy formulation consists of three stages, namely, mission, evolution and strategy. A state or middle level initiative deals with synchronisation, infrastructure and organisation that are needed to overcome the barriers to implementation. Finally, a bottom up or local level initiative of monitoring and evaluation provides strategy control as a process of adaptive management.

Figure 6.2: Systemic Approach to Maritime Affairs

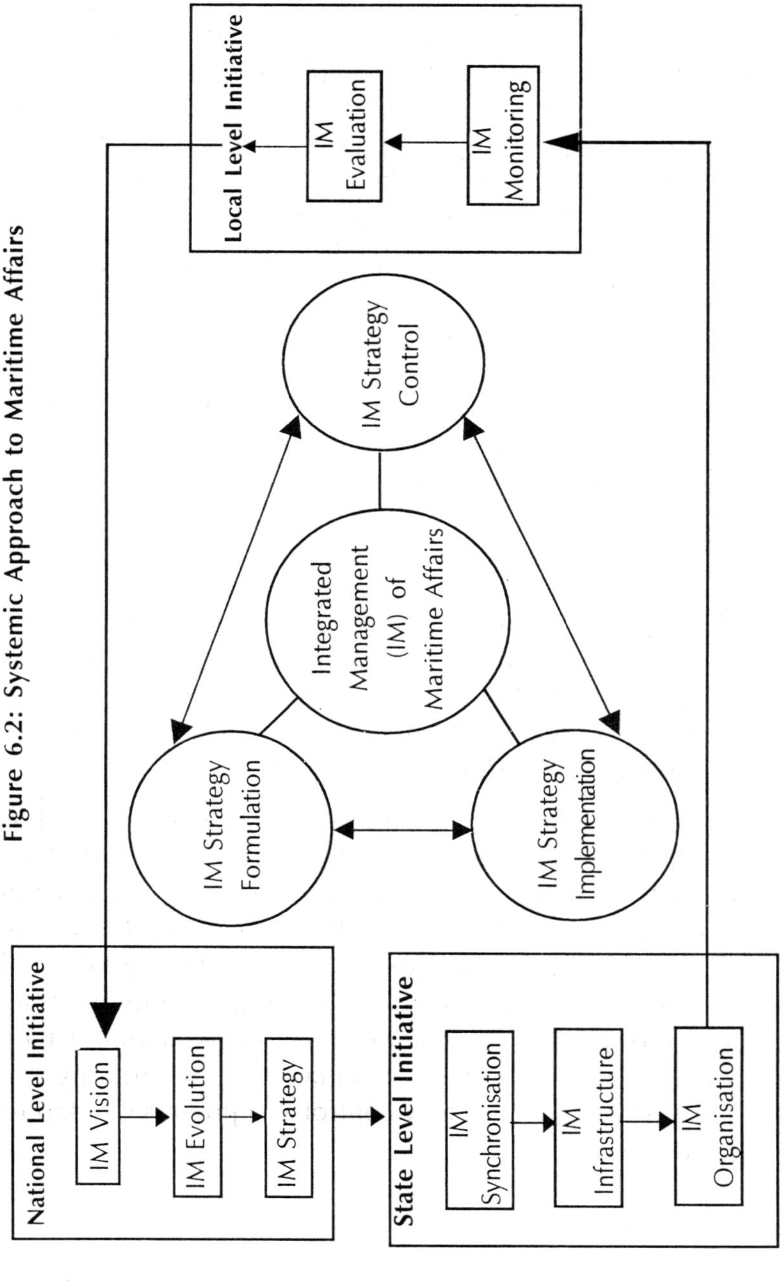

## Strategy Formulation

In Figure 6.3, the what, why, who and where of strategy formulation depicts the mission by categorising intentions that are broad, all inclusive and forward thinking. In examining "what" is being sought, the mission identifies that a collaborative, cooperative and coordinated approach amongst the sectoral policy makers, other stakeholders and project actors, would in terms of expected outcomes achieve sustainable development, economic efficiency and improve not only the quality of life but also of the marine environment. In addressing, "who" are the entities the mission inspires commitment by synthesising policy makers, other stakeholders and project actors. As to "why" is there a need to initiate integrated management the mission provides a shared purpose, which describes the aspirations for the future without specifying the means that will be used. Finally, looking at "where" the applications are located the mission is challenging in attempting to integrate the national, state and local levels of governance.

The mission redefines the role of the government organisation in the economy and a change in the corporate culture of bureaucracy. To realise the mission at the national level, one has to understand the emergence of the innovative organisation (in the previous chapter) from the traditional bureaucratic organisation. The six basic parts of an organisation (Mintzberg, in Mintzberg and Quinn, 1998): strategic apex, middle line, operating core, technostructure, support staff and ideology, can be related to the bureaucratic system of management that exists in India. The strategic apex (Prime Minister), middle line (Cabinet) and the flat operating core (Government Ministries/Departments) are typically connected through a single chain of formal authority. The technostructure

**Figure 6.3: Integrated Management Mission**

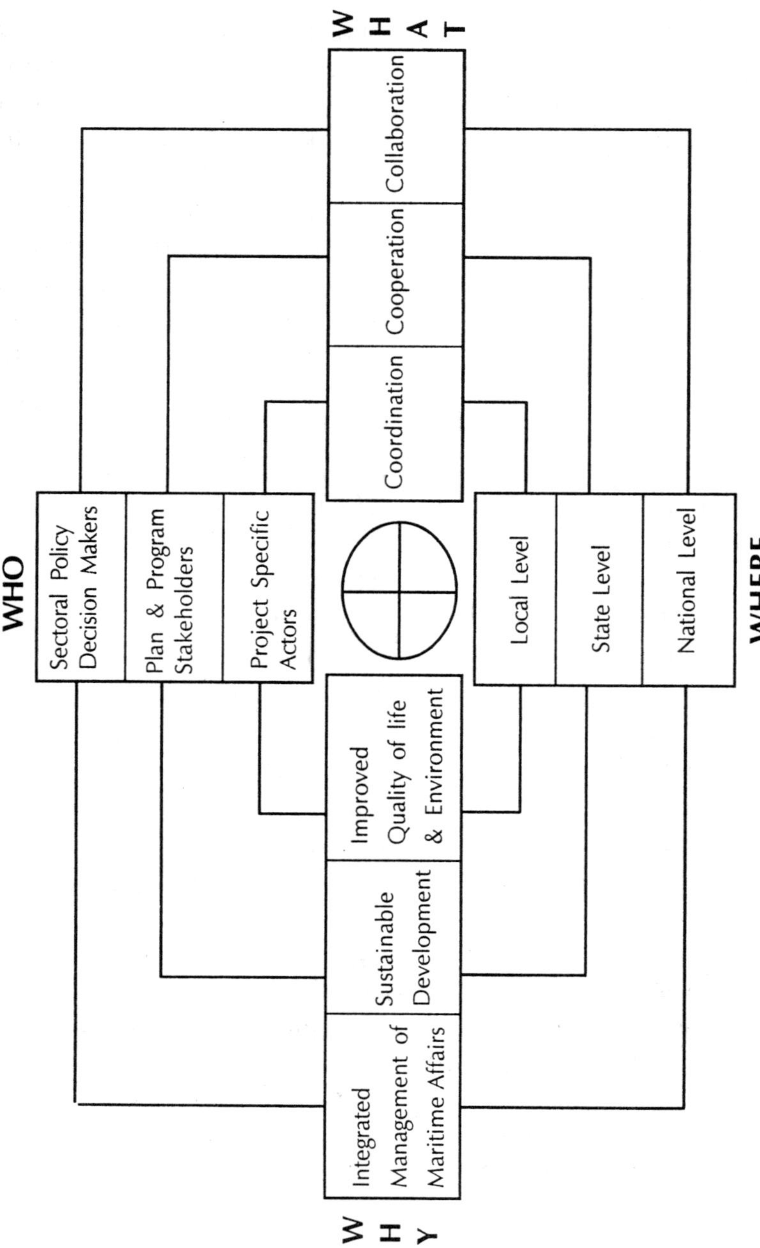

(Research and Development, scientific and academic institutions) and the supporting staff (administrative staff) influence the operating core indirectly. The ideology of the system of management is based on a tall authority structure - political system superimposed on the bureaucratic structure - with multiple reporting levels and a decision making apparatus that concentrates authority near the top (Gupta and Fletcher, 2000). Thinking is delegated to the professional and doing is accomplished in a collection of functionally distinct departments populated by professional individuals who are focussed on specialised and generally fragmented tasks (Ostroff, 1999).

The traditional bureaucratic organisation inhibits creativity and initiative of better-educated employer coupled with advances in information technology. Management layers often add to overhead costs with standardised procedures and inflexible plans slowing response times in a complex and dynamic marine environment. Hence, traditional bureaucratic organisations are unable to deliver in terms of differentiation, cost leadership and response time compared to emerging lively, dynamic and constantly evolving organic organisations. In pursuing the theme that there are ties which unite strategy and structure, four configurations emerge that relate the niche differentiation:- cost leadership, innovative differentiation and conglomeration strategies to the entrepreneurial, machine, innovative and diversified organisations (Miller, in Segal-Horn, 1998). In the maritime zone, rapid adaptation to the dynamic environment is essential. The innovation context is one in which the organisation must deal with complex systems under conditions of dynamic change (Miller, in Segal-Horn, 1998). Integrated Management can, thus, be viewed as akin to the innovative differentiation strategy. Table 6.1 outlines the summary of the structural dimensions and the favoured strategy.

## Table 6.1: Structure and Strategy Fits

| Structural Dimensions | Entrepreneurial Organisation | Machine Organisation | Innotive Organisation | Diversified Organisation |
|---|---|---|---|---|
| **Power Centralisation** | All at the top | CEO and designers of workflow | Scientists, technocrats and middle managers | Divisional executives |
| **Bureau-cratisation** | Low-informal | Many formal rules, policies and procedures | Organic | Bureaucratic |
| **Specialisation** | Low | Extensive | Extensive | Extensive |
| **Differentiation** | Minimal | Moderate | Very high | High |
| **Competition** | Extreme | High | Moderate | Varies |
| **Dynamism/ Uncertainty** | Moderate | Very low | Very high | Varies |
| **Growth** | Varies | Slow | Rapid | Varies |
| **Information Systems** | Crude, informal | Cost controls and budget | Informal scanning, open communications | Management information systems and profit centres |
| **Integration and co-ordination of effort** | By CEO via direct supervision | By technocrat via formal procedures | By integrating personnel, task forces via mutual adjustment | By formal committees via plans and budgets |
| **Favoured Strategy** | Niche differentiation | Cost leadership | Innovative differentiation | Conglomeration |

*Source:* Miller, in Segal Horn 1998

**Figure 6.4: Integrated Management Evolution**

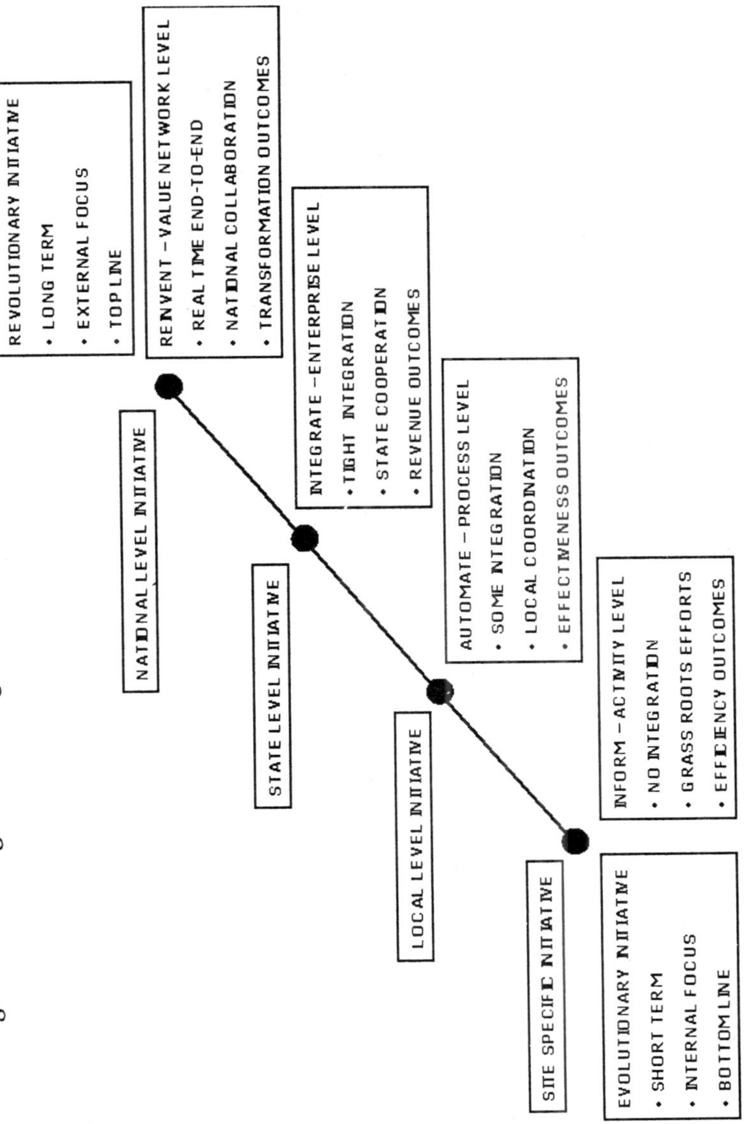

In the complex and dynamic marine environment, there is a need to adjust strategy continually as it is put into place. It is, therefore, not possible to separate strategy formulation from strategy implementation leading to overlap in policy formulation and implementation in a process known as "learning by doing" or "organisational learning" in strategic management. Organisational learning assumes a middle ground between rational planning or deliberate strategies and incremental or emergent strategies. Drawing from Mintzberg, purely deliberate strategy based on rational planning suggests no learning. In addition, emergent strategies based on incremental strategies suggest no control. In the real world of management of maritime affairs there is a need for organisational learning that mixes these characteristics. The rational planning perspective of individual sectors develops a deliberate strategy. Organisational learning through a process of collaboration, cooperation and coordination allows the organisation to develop an emergent strategy incrementally to control its sectoral deliberate strategy. The process of organisational learning can be evolutionary or revolutionary (Figure 6.4).

An evolutionary bottom level initiative is in the short term with an internal focus. While the revolutionary top line initiative is in the long term with an external focus. The organisation may start at any of the activity, process, enterprise or value network levels. The activity level is a grass roots effort focussed on efficiency outcomes at the site level with no integration and informing the organisational project actors. The process level is a local coordinating body effort focussed on effectiveness outcomes at the local level with some level of integration and automating the management programme. The enterprise level is a state coordinating body effort focussed on resource outcomes at the state level with tight integration and also integrating the management organisational plan. The value network level is a national coordinating body effort with a focus on transformation outcomes at the national level, with real time end-to-end network and reinventing the management organisational policy. A review of the ocean and coastal management literature indicates that an evolutionary or grass roots initiative invariably requires national level support for it to be sustained. Hence, the process of organisational learning needs a combination of top-down and bottom up approach for integrated management.

Maritime affairs involve management decisions that are complex in a dynamic environment. The decision demands coupled with the complexity inevitably leads to sectoral conflict that is irresolvable. The source of dynamic complexity with emphasis on connections and interrelationships lies in the multiple stakeholders, numerous sectors, deeply ingrained values, cultural differences, scientific knowledge, legal requirements, competition for the same ocean space and the entrenched conflict industry. Integrated management through a process of systemic thinking can improve the situation by mutual learning that allows resolving specific conflicts. Ludwig Von Bertalanffy, who defines a system as a complex of interacting elements first formulated the concept. The systems approach, demonstrates in its sheer substance the tangibility and prominence of wholes, which are dynamic by nature and not just the sum of basic elements. Figure 6.5 identifies a set of elements and processes for configuring a systemic strategy for maritime management. The elements are the interacting components that define the system for management. The approach responds to dynamic complexity in maritime affairs by true integrative thinking that can manipulate mental models to explore relationships and possibilities.

Figure 6.5: Configuring Integrated Management Strategy

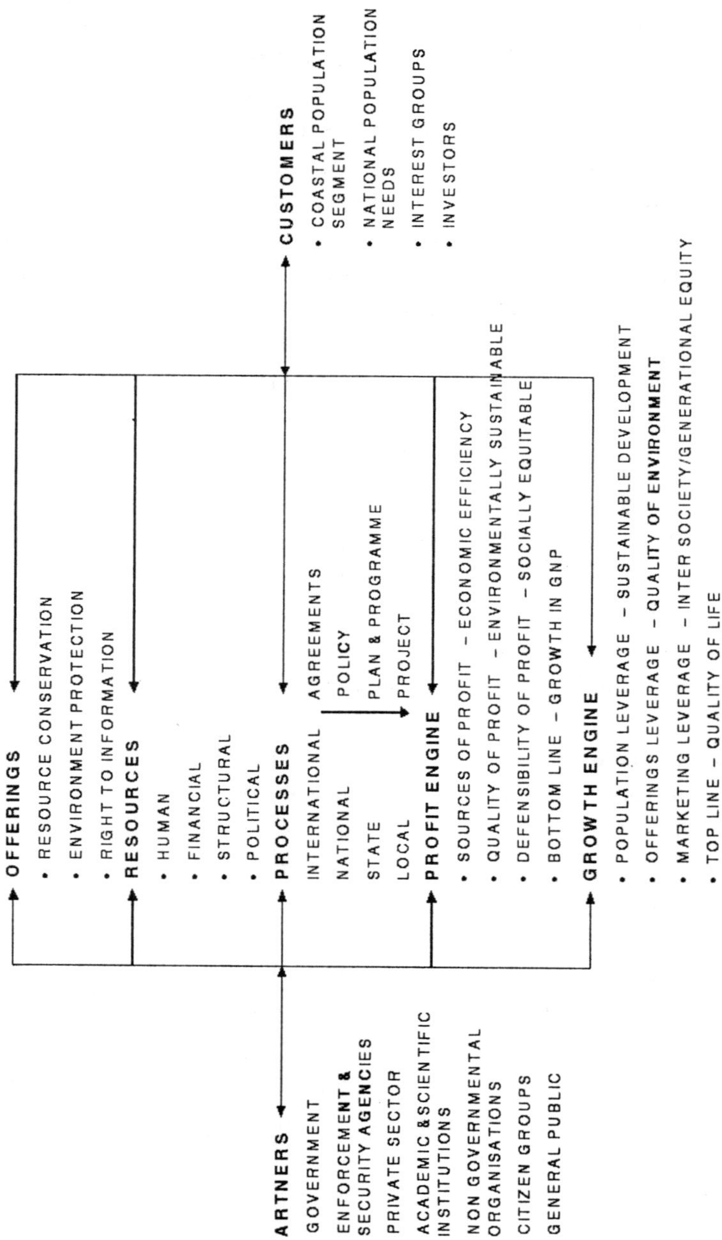

There are several technical and political difficulties in integrating the economic, environmental and security objectives to adequately address the inter-sectoral dimensions of maritime affairs. Activities in the maritime sector cannot be dealt with on an ad hoc or piece meal basis. It is becoming increasingly evident that there exists a need to build national capability in maritime strategy policy making and planning. This implies new ways of thinking and working so as to move from developing and implementing a fixed plan, which gets increasingly outmoded towards operating an adaptive system that can continuously evolve and improve. It also implies that it is not the state alone that is responsible for development; the responsibility also lies with the society as a whole. A centralised and controlled decision making process towards sharing results and opportunities, transparent negotiation, cooperation and concerted action would also be desirable. It would mean not just a focus on outputs (projects and laws) alone, but also a focus on outcomes (impacts) and the quality of participation and management processes. Thus, one could advance from sectoral planning towards integrated planning. Costly projects consequently casing dependence on external assistance could be converted to domestically driven and financed development.

The approach to strategy formulation cannot be a one-of initiative but needs to be a coordinated and continuously improving processes of analysis, debate, capacity-strengthening, planning and investment, which integrates the economic, environmental and security objectives of a maritime activity, seeking workable solutions where this is not possible. This entails the identification, coordination and continuous improvement of mechanisms that can help towards balancing the economic, environmental and security concerns of multiple stakeholders.

## Strategy Implementation

The process of strategy implementation needs blending of perspectives and coordinating a broad range of efforts aimed at transforming the strategic intent into action. For individual maritime sectors to become willing participants, fundamental changes in how people think and act are required to shape the context within which sectoral departments or people go about their everyday business. Strategy implementation, is inextricably connected with organisational change. The organisation to make progress towards change entails two levels - adaptive and generative in what has been called as a punctuated equilibrium model. Principles of management reinforced through international experience requires the organisational model to consist of an operating core for issue identification, an administrative component to set policy direction, a strategic apex or political leadership to provide the mission, a coordinating mechanism to allow open communication of ideas and information and an advisory group for assessment, feedback and acting as a node information dissemination and identification of gaps in knowledge. This requires a change in ideology to a more decentralised approach to management. Decentralisation means the diffusion of decision making power. Synchronising the leadership, administrative and operating levels of governance through a coordinating mechanism and an advisory group allows for adaptive and generative changes. The coordinating mechanism is incremental and evolutionary in nature; analogous to "working in the system" by coordinating day-to-day organisational transactions and is not aimed at organisational transformation. The advisory group by networking specialised people is a quantum breakthrough and analogous to "working on the system." These paradigm shifts in the method of governance constitutes the adaptive and generative organisational changes.

In the process of moving from strategy formulation at the national level to strategy implementation at the state level, expanding on the 7-S model developed by Mckinsey and Company, Figure 6.6 illustrates the synchronisation of strategic change that needs to be addressed.

The expanded 7-S model can be aligned to Allaire's organisational architecture of hard and soft elements of organisational context. Strategy, systems, structure, sourcing and staffing are the hard elements, while shared values, style, skills and synergy are the soft elements. Taken together these nine elements are the enablers to change.

**Figure 6.6: Integrated Management Synchronisation**

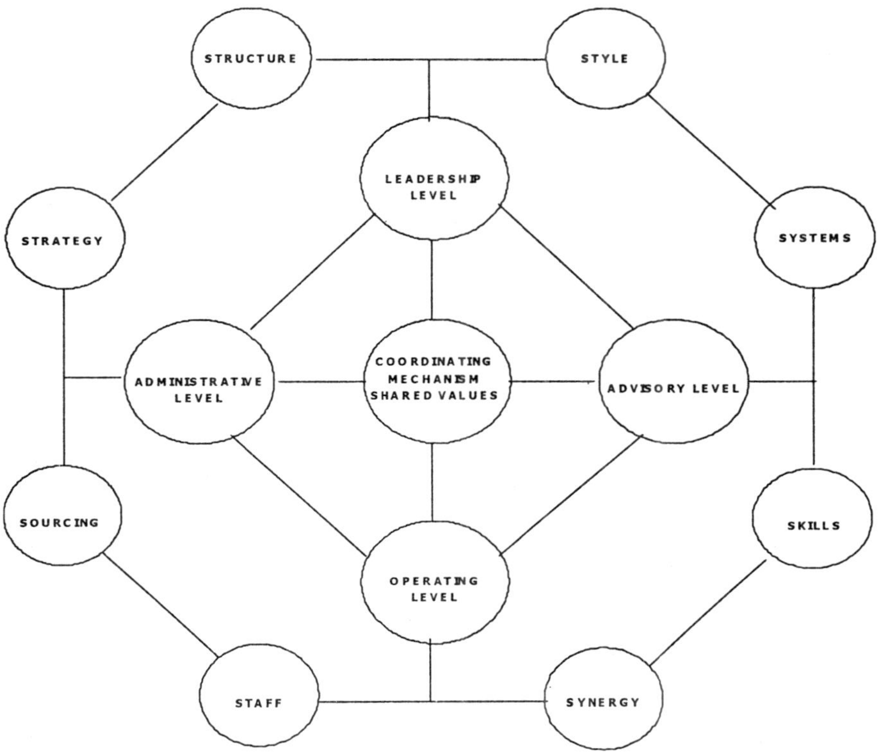

**Table 6.2: Integrated Management Enablers of Change**

| Enabler | Change |
|---|---|
| **Strategy** | The plan for allocating the organisations resources to achieve its goals |
| **Systems** | The administrative procedures, routines, and information systems that characterise how work is done in the organisation |
| **Structure** | The way the organisation's units relate to each other, including formal reporting and authority relationships |
| **Staff** | The numbers, levels, and types of people employed in the organisation |
| **Style** | Patterns of behaviour of key managers in achieving the organisation's goals |
| **Skills** | Distinctive capabilities of key personnel of organisation as a whole |
| **Synergy** | Coordination between sectors and across all levels of the organisation |
| **Sourcing** | Mobilising resources for funding development plans relates to the ability of the organisation to identify and tap resources |
| **Shared Values** | The significant meanings, guiding concepts, core values, core purpose, and aspirations, often unwritten, that go beyond the conventional formal statement of organisational objectives |

Experience shows that organisations in trying to maintain status quo and resisting change, because of the deeply ingrained mental models, have a cascading effect on the hard and soft elements of context that fuel organisational excellence. However, when fundamental change becomes necessary, the organisation has to be able to pull apart through the competitive force of politics. Thus, the success of strategy implementation depends upon political will in overcoming the inertia to change. It is ironic that an organisation with an unified approach to strategy requires action at an individual level; only a powerful political force may be strong enough to cause a break with the past thinking and allow for a new order to emerge.

The current marine environment – with its multiple stakeholders, interdependent sectors, constantly changing data and information, and increasing complexity – requires a networked approach. Information and knowledge network that supports collaboration, cooperation and coordination lacks the desired strategic direction just as the capacity to change embedded in mindsets. Information (data + context) and knowledge (information + insight) bases are essential to strategy implementation as it allows decision makers to take informed and knowledgeable decisions. Conceptually, the infrastructure – in terms of the key entities that surround the strategy implementation process and the applications that connect them – would have to be interlinked. The development of an Enterprise Resource Planning (ERP) integration backbone (Figure 6.7) promotes understanding amongst the stakeholders and across the economic maritime sectors by taking short and long-term views for sustainable development of the land-sea interface, and beyond.

**Figure 6.7: Integrated Management Infrastructure**

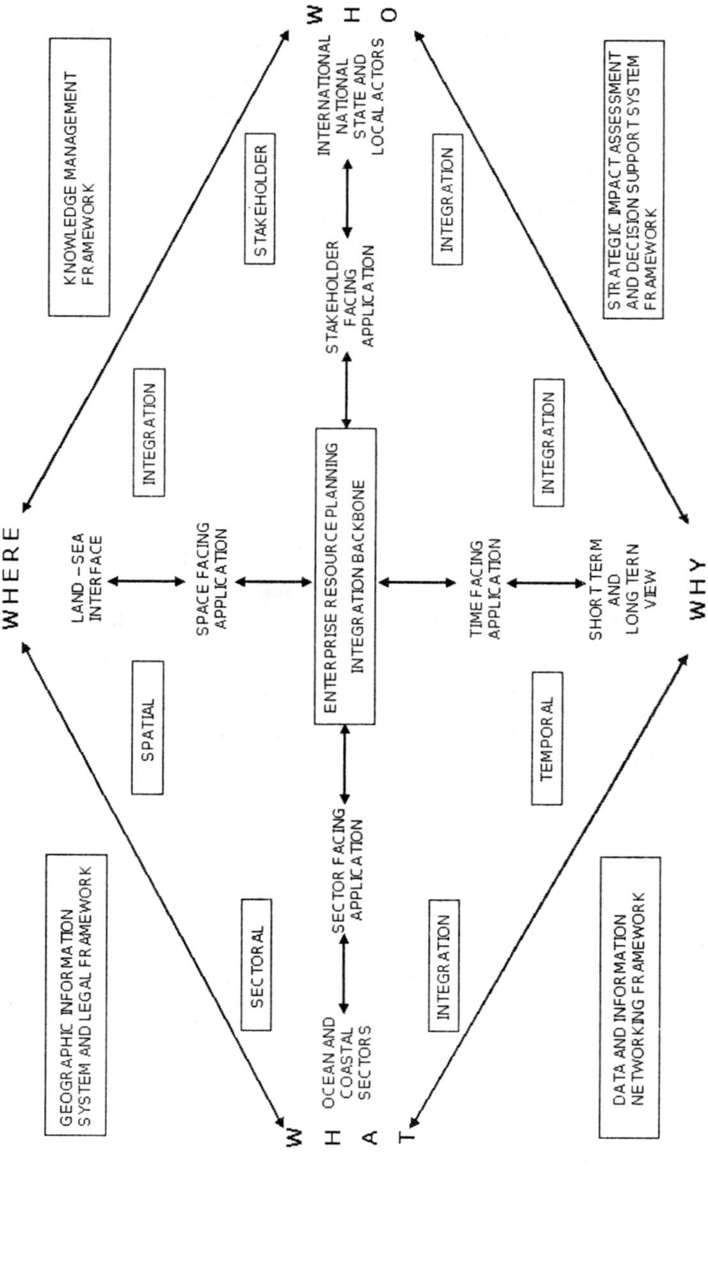

It allows information and knowledge to be centralised and shared across boundaries and multiple functional areas. The processes involved in strategically managing relationships between stakeholders and sectors over time and space are interconnected and interdependent. Therefore, the applications that enable these processes are also integrated and interdependent.

A successful outcome for integrated management may be seen as dependent on (Gupta and Fletcher, 2000):

a) Establishing a 'language of change', one that all stakeholders can speak and understand.

b) Establishing a management framework capable of adapting to the dynamic macro-environment and continually changing socio-cultural situation.

c) A flexible planning system consisting of education and research components which cuts across scientific disciplines.

The elements of organisational redesign must, therefore, logically configure into its internally consistent groupings (Mintzberg, in Mintzberg and Quinn, 1998). Figure 6.8 provides a reflection of the mechanisms needed for organisational redesign for strategy implementation.

## Strategy Control

Finally, to execute the strategy is to execute change at all levels of the organisational framework. Strategy control requires evaluation indicators at the local level for monitoring the implementation and informing policy makers of the effectiveness of the strategy. The use of the Balanced Scorecard to turn strategy into action allows creating a Strategy-Focused Organisation (Kaplan and Norton, 2000). The Balanced Scorecard translates

**Figure 6.8: Integrated Management Organisation**

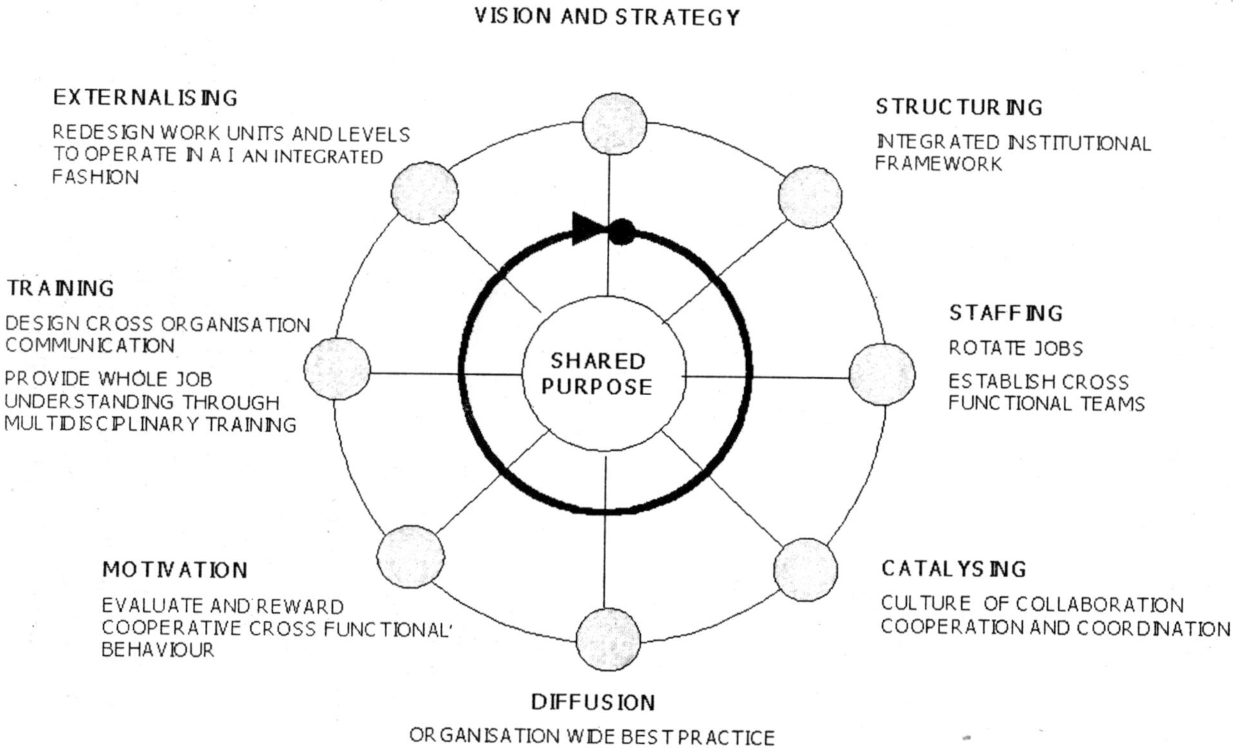

the strategy to operational terms and ensures that meeting the goals of integrated management strategy is everyone's job, and a continual process. The Balanced Scorecard (Table 6.3) allows determining critical parameters across the economic, internal management, stakeholder, innovations and operations perspective and provides the requisite indicators of initiative across the leadership, process, culture, measurement and technology spectrums.

The Balanced Scorecard as an evaluation and monitoring tool allows translating the mission into a plan for implementation which is communicated to link the stakeholders who in turn learn and provide feedback using a data and information network. As a measure of effectiveness what is needed is a Maritime Quotient (MQ) similar to that shown in Figure 6.9. A MQ score is an overall number that can be used to track progress in implementing the management of maritime affairs. MQ can be calculated at multiple levels of the management process from individual sectors to cross-sectoral performance and within ministries and departments. For arriving at the MQ we can use the elements of the Balanced Scorecard namely criteria, initiative, success factors and critical measurements to arrive at an overall score.

How does this all work? What does the management of maritime affairs life cycle look like? Figure 6.10 summaries the life cycle process in the management of maritime affairs.

**Table 6.3: Integrated Management Monitoring and Evaluation**

| | **Financial Perspective** | **Management Perspective** | **Stakeholder Perspective** | **Innovation Perspective** | **Operations Perspective** |
|---|---|---|---|---|---|
| **IM Complimentary Criteria** | Translating IM vision | Planning and implementation | Communicating and linking | Learning & Feedback | Data & Information Network |
| **IM Initiative** | **Leadership to IM** | **IM Process** | **IM Culture** | **IM Measurement** | **IM Technology** |
| **Success Factors** | * Growth in GNP<br>* Economically efficient development<br>* Environmentally sustainable development<br>* Socially equitable development | * Long term view<br>* Organising around an integrated approach<br>* Collaborative culture<br>* Coordinated policies and regulations | * Shared costs<br>* Better communication<br>* Accessibility to information<br>* Public participation in decision making | * Development of best practice<br>* Development of understanding through multidisciplinary training<br>* Development of conflict resolution mechanism | * All stakeholders networked<br>* Establishment of a central repository for data collection of dissemination |
| **Critical Measurements** | * Output of Ocean & Coastal activity vis-à-vis GNP<br>* Quality of life<br>* Quality of environment<br>* Extent of inter-society & inter-generational equity | * Careful decision making<br>* Extent of networking amongst sectoral line agencies<br>* Level of stakeholder participation<br>* National law in conformity with international legislation | * Development costs– before vs after<br>* Awareness level of decision makers<br>* Frequency of accessing information by stakeholders<br>* Level of local involvement | * Indicators defined to measure goals<br>* Extent of strategic impact assessment<br>* Level of adaptive management | * Level of stakeholder integration into the network<br>* Extent of data sharing by individual stakeholders<br>* Extent of transforming data into knowledge |

**Figure 6.9: Integrated Management Measure of Effectiveness**

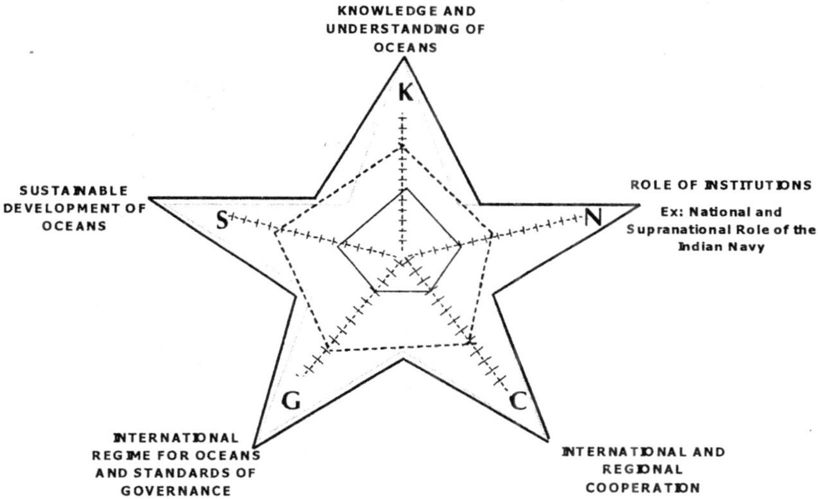


Source: Adapted from Shankar, 2001

Essentially, the life cycle for management of maritime affairs entails, firstly, developing a maritime outlook that defines the maritime resource of India's power - maritime power in accordance with international obligations and national objectives. Besides, (step 2) it includes identifying the objectives and outcomes in terms of the political implications of all international agreements relating to the maritime zones, the economic potential of the maritime sector, the environmental goals for the maritime zone, the social and cultural regions, the technological advancement needed for sustainable development of maritime activities, and the changing security concerns in our maritime zone, and in the wider ambit of the Indian Ocean. It necessitates balancing the objectives using the Maritime Quotient and defining an overall score to be achieved as a target (step 3). Developing and adopting an action plan for implementation would also be required (step 4).

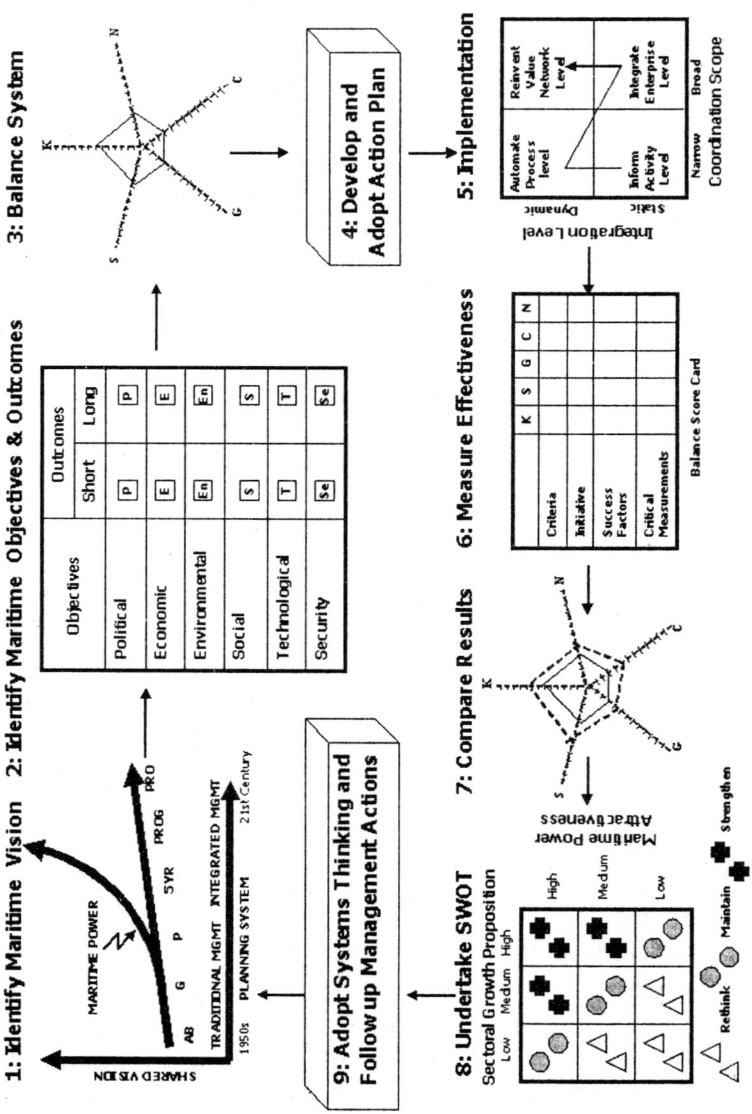


Figure 6.10: Management of Maritime Affairs Life Cycle

The process of implementation can be evolutionary or revolutionary (step 5). This would involve developing and using the balanced scorecard to measure the targets (step 6). It would also include comparing the results with the original targets (step 7), and undertaking a Strengths, Weaknesses, Opportunities and Threats (SWOT) analysis of the maritime power attractiveness versus sectoral growth projection (step 8). Finally, one would adopt a systemic approach and simulate findings using a software model (such as the Ithink software) and follow up with resultant management actions.

Can this national maritime vision be realised? The answer is, yes. Political commitment at the national and state levels is central to the answer for an effective strategy, notably to ensure development rather than narrow sectoral viewpoints. It would underpin appreciation that there are several intertwined issues that need to be addressed in terms of their physical, social, economic, financial, environmental, technical, and security implications to enable the strategy coordination system to work effectively. This would ensure that the policy implications of the strategy are followed and considered throughout the process and not merely at some formal end-point. Decisions would be made on recommended policy and institutional changes, ensuring that changes are introduced and followed through. Government departments would need to be intimated that relevant polices, plans and procedures should be coordinated amongst the stakeholders prior to committing government funds. This would mean keeping the strategy process open and inclusive and not confidential and closed, thus, encouraging participation in the strategy, giving participants ready access to information, and encouraging them to adopt critical approaches.

Most strategies have failed because of weak government understanding, leadership and overall commitment. The road map defines the rules and norms for integrated management of maritime affairs. Working in this way requires a preparedness to work in a different way from those that have generally prevailed to date. The proposed three-tier structure is already prevalent within the government. What the road map does is, it highlights the specific initiatives needed at the three essential levels of management. The initiatives at the national or top level management concerned with strategy formulation relate to formulating an inspirational, aspiring and challenging maritime policy, establishing its process of evolution and configuring the strategy for implementation. The state or middle level management responsible for strategy implementation needs to first synchronise the strategy to an organic organisational framework, create the infrastructure for managing knowledge and develop a shared purpose over the short and long term within the organisation. Finally, it emerges that although the strategy may be formulated and adopted at the top, the actual execution is from below by the local Panchayati Raj institutions or bottom level management initiative.

# Appendix 1

## List of Landlocked Countries

| S.No | Landlocked Country | Connected Ocean/Seas | Tranship Seaport | Country |
|---|---|---|---|---|
| | **Asia Pacific** | | | |
| 1 | Afghanistan | Indian Ocean | Karachi | Pakistan |
| 2 | Bhutan | Indian Ocean | Kolkota | India |
| 3 | Kyrgyzstan | Baltic Sea | St Petersburg | Russia |
| 4 | Laos | South China Sea | Bangkok | Thailand |
| 5 | Mongolia | South China Sea<br>Sea of Japan | | China<br>Russia |
| 6 | Nepal | Indian Ocean | Mumbai<br>Kolkota | India |
| 7 | Tajikistan | Indian Ocean | Karachi | Pakistan |
| 8 | Uzbekistan | Black Sea<br>Baltic Sea | Batumi<br>St Petersburg | Georgia<br>Russia |
| 9 | Azerbaijan | Black Sea<br>Baltic Sea | Batumi<br>St Petersburg | Georgia<br>Russia |
| 10 | Kazakstan | Black Sea<br>Baltic Sea | Batumi<br>St Petersburg | Gerorgia<br>Russia |
| 11 | Turkmenistan | Black Sea<br>Baltic Sea | Batumi<br>St Petersburg | Gerorgia<br>Russia |

| S.No | Landlocked Country | Connected Ocean/Seas | Tranship Seaport | Country |
|---|---|---|---|---|
| | **Africa** | | | |
| 12 | Botswana | Indian Ocean | Durban | South Africa |
| 13 | Burkina Faso | Atlantic Ocean | Abidjan | Côte d'Ivoire |
| 14 | Burundi | Atlantic Ocean<br>Indian Ocean | Matadi<br>Dar es Salaam | Congo<br>Tanzania |
| 15 | Central African Republic | Atlantic Ocean | Douala<br>Matadi<br>Pointe Noire | Cameroon<br>Congo<br>Congo |
| 16 | Chad | Atlantic Ocean | Douala | Cameroon |
| 17 | Ethiopia | Indian Ocean | | Eritrea |
| 18 | Lesotho | Indian Ocean | Durban | South Africa |
| 19 | Malawi | Indian Ocean | Nacala | Mozambique |
| 20 | Mali | Atlantic Ocean | Abidjan<br>Conakry<br>Dakar | Côte d'Ivoire<br>Guinea<br>Senegal |
| 21 | Niger | Atlantic Ocean | Cotonou | Benin |
| 22 | Rwanda | Indian Ocean | Dar es Salaam<br>Mombasa | Tanzania<br>Kenya |
| 23 | Swaziland | Indian Ocean | Durban | South Africa |
| 24 | Uganda | Indian Ocean | Mombasa<br>Tanga | Kenya<br>Tanzania |
| 25 | Zambia | Indian Ocean | Dar es Salaam | Tanzania |
| 26 | Zimbabwe | Indian Ocean | Beira<br>Durban | Mozambique<br>South Africa |

| S.No | Landlocked Country | Connected Ocean/Seas | Tranship Seaport | Country |
|---|---|---|---|---|
| | **Europe** | | | |
| 27 | Andorra | Mediterranean Sea | Barcelona | Spain |
| 28 | Armenia | Black Sea | Batumi | Georgia |
| | | Mediterranean Sea | Mersin | Turkey |
| 29 | Austria | English Channel | Antwerp | Belgium |
| | | North Sea | Hamburg | Germany |
| | | | Rotterdam | Netherlands |
| | | Mediterranean Sea | Marseilles | France |
| 30 | Belarus | Baltic Sea | Gdansk | Gdynia |
| | | | Gdynia | Poland |
| | | | St Petersburg | Russia |
| | | Black Sea | Odessa | Ukraine |
| 31 | Bosnia and Herzegovina | Adriatic Sea | — | Croatia |
| 32 | Czech Republic | Baltic Sea | Gdansk | Poland |
| | | | Gdynia | Poland |
| | | | Szczecin | Poland |
| | | | Hamburg | Germany |
| 33 | Hungary | English Channel | Antwerp | Belgium |
| | | North Sea | Hamburg | Germany |
| | | | Rotterdam | Netherlands |
| 34 | Liechtenstein | English Channel | Antwerp | Belgium |
| | | North Sea | Hamburg | Germany |
| | | | Rotterdam | Netherlands |
| | | Mediterranean Sea | Marseilles | France |
| 35 | Luxembourg | English Channel | Antwerp | Belgium |
| 36 | Republic of Moldova | Black Sea | Odessa | Ukraine |

| S.No | Landlocked Country | Connected Ocean/Seas | Tranship Seaport | Asia Pacific |
|---|---|---|---|---|
| 37 | San Marino | Adriatic Sea | — | Italy |
| 38 | Slovakia | Baltic Sea | Gdansk | Poland |
| | | Baltic Sea | Gdynia | Poland |
| | | | Szczecin | Poland |
| 39 | Switzerland | English Channel | Antwerp | Belgium |
| | | | Le Havre | France |
| | | North Sea | Hamburg | Germany |
| | | | Rotterdam | Netherlands |
| | | Mediterranean Sea | Genoa | Italy |
| | | | Marseilles | France |
| 40 | The Former Yugoslav Republic of Macedonia | Adriatic Sea | Durrés | Albania |
| | | Aegean Sea | Istanbul | Turkey |
| | | Black Sea | Varna | Bulgaria |
| | **Americas** | | | |
| 41 | Bolivia | Pacific Ocean | Arica | Chile |
| | | | Matarani | Peru |
| | | Atlantic Ocean | Buenos Aires | Argentina |
| | | | Santos | Brazil |
| 42 | Paraguay | Atlantic Ocean | Buenos Aires | Argentina |
| | | | Santos | Brazil |

*Sources:*

1. Export 911 Shipping Department website http://www.export911.com/e911/ship/landlock.htm
2. United Nations Conference on Trade and Development list of Landlocked Countries
3. What you need to know about Geography website http://geography.about.com/library/weekly/aa042699.htm

Appendix 2

# List of Indian Ocean Countries

| S.No | Country | Date of UN Membership |
|---|---|---|
| **South East Asia and Malacca Straits** | | |
| 1 | Australia | 01 Nov 1945 |
| 2 | Indonesia | 28 Sep 1950 |
| 3 | Myanmar | 19 Apr 1948 |
| 4 | Malaysia | 17 Sep 1957 |
| 5 | Singapore | 21 Sep 1965 |
| 6 | Thailand | 16 Dec 1946 |
| **South Asia** | | |
| 7 | Afghanistan | 19 Nov 1946 |
| 8 | Bangladesh | 17 Sep 1974 |
| 9 | Bhutan | 21 Sep 1971 |
| 10 | India | 30 Oct 1945 |
| 11 | Nepal | 14 Dec 1955 |
| 12 | Pakistan | 30 Sep 1947 |
| 13 | Sri Lanka | 14 Dec 1955 |

| S.No | Country | Date of UN Membership |
|---|---|---|
| **Persian Gulf** | | |
| 14 | Bahrain | 21 Sep 1971 |
| 15 | Iran | 24 Oct 1945 |
| 16 | Iraq | 21 Dec 1945 |
| 17 | Kuwait | 14 May 1963 |
| 18 | Oman | 07 Oct 1971 |
| 19 | Qatar | 21 Sep 1971 |
| 20 | Saudi Arabia | 24 Oct 1945 |
| 21 | United Arab Emirates | 09 Dec 1971 |
| **Horn of Africa and Red Sea** | | |
| 22 | Djibouti | 20 Sep 1977 |
| 23 | Egypt | 24 Oct 1945 |
| 24 | Ethopia | 13 Nov 1945 |
| 25 | Eritrea | 28 May 1993 |
| 26 | Israel | 11 May 1949 |
| 27 | Jordan | 14 Dec 1955 |
| 28 | Somalia | 20 Sep 1960 |
| 29 | Sudan | 12 Nov 1956 |
| 30 | Yemen | 30 Sep 1947 |
| **Eastern and Southern Africa** | | |
| 31 | Botswana | 17 Oct 1966 |
| 32 | Burundi | 18 Sep 1962 |
| 33 | Kenya | 16 Dec 1963 |

| | | |
|---|---|---|
| 34 | Lesotho | 17 Oct 1966 |
| 35 | Malawi | 01 Dec 1964 |
| 36 | Mozambique | 16 Sep 1975 |
| 37 | Rwanda | 18 Sep 1962 |
| 38 | South Africa | 07 Nov 1945 |
| 39 | Swaziland | 24 Sep 1968 |
| 40 | Tanzania | 14 Dec 1961 |
| 41 | Uganda | 25 Oct 1962 |
| 42 | Zambia | 01 Dec 1964 |
| 43 | Zimbabwe | 25 Aug 1980 |
| 44 | Comoros | 12 Nov 1975 |
| 45 | Madagascar | 20 Sep 1960 |
| 46 | Maldives | 21 Sep 1965 |
| 47 | Mauritius | 07 Oct 1964 |
| 48 | Seychelles | 21 Sep 1976 |

**Other Island Territories**

49 Ashmore & Cartier Islands (AS)

50 Bassas da India (FR)

51 British Indian Ocean Territory [Chagos] (UK)

52 Christmas Island (AS)

53 Cocos (Keeling) Islands (AS)

54 Europa Island (FR)

55 French Southern & Antarctic Islands (FR)

56 Glorioso Islands (FR)

| S.No | Country | Date of UN Membership |
|---|---|---|
| 57 | Heard Is. & McDonald Isles (AS) | |
| 58 | Juan de Nova Island (FR) | |
| 59 | Mayotte (FR) | |
| 60 | Reunion (FR) | |
| 61 | Tromelin Island (FR) | |
| **Central Asian Republics** | | |
| 62 | Kazakhstan | 02 Mar 1992 |
| 63 | Kyrgyzstan | 02 Mar 1992 |
| 64 | Tajikistan | 02 Mar 1992 |
| 65 | Turkmenistan | 02 mar 1992 |
| 66 | Uzbekistan | 02 Mar 1992 |

# Appendix 3

## India's Maritime States

| S. no. | Coastal State/ Union | Length of Coastline | no. of Districts | Area in KM$^2$ | Population (2001) | Density per KM$^2$ |
|---|---|---|---|---|---|---|
| | **WEST COAST MAINLAND** | | | | | |
| 1 | Gujarat | 1214.7 | 25 | 1,96,024 | 50,596,992 | 258 |
| 2 | Daman & Diu | 42.5 | 02 | 112 | 158,059 | 1,411 |
| 3 | Maharashtra | 652.6 | 35 | 3,07,713 | 96,752,247 | 314 |
| 4 | Goa | 118.0 | 02 | 3,702 | 1,343,998 | 363 |
| 5 | Karnataka | 280.0 | 27 | 1,91,791 | 52,733,958 | 275 |
| 6 | Kerala | 280.0 | 27 | 1,91,791 | 52,733,958 | 275 |
| | **EAST COAST MAINLAND** | | | | | |
| 7 | West Bengal | 157.5 | 18 | 88,752 | 80,221,171 | 904 |
| 8 | Orissa | 476.4 | 30 | 1,55,707 | 36706,920 | 236 |
| 9 | Andhra Pradesh | 973.7 | 23 | 2,75,045 | 75,706,920 | 236 |
| 10 | Tamil Nadu | 906.9 | 30 | 1,30,058 | 62,110,839 | 478 |
| 11 | Pondicherry(UT) | 30.6 | 04 | 492 | 973,829 | 2,029 |
| | **ISLAND TERRITORIES** | | | | | |
| 12 | Lakshwadeep & Minicoy(UT) | 132.0 | 01 | 32 | 60,595 | 1,894 |
| 13 | Andaman & Nicobar | 1962.0 | 02 | 8,249 | 356,265 | 43 |
| **14** | **Total** | **7516.6** | **213** | **1,396,540** | **489,581,033** | **350** |

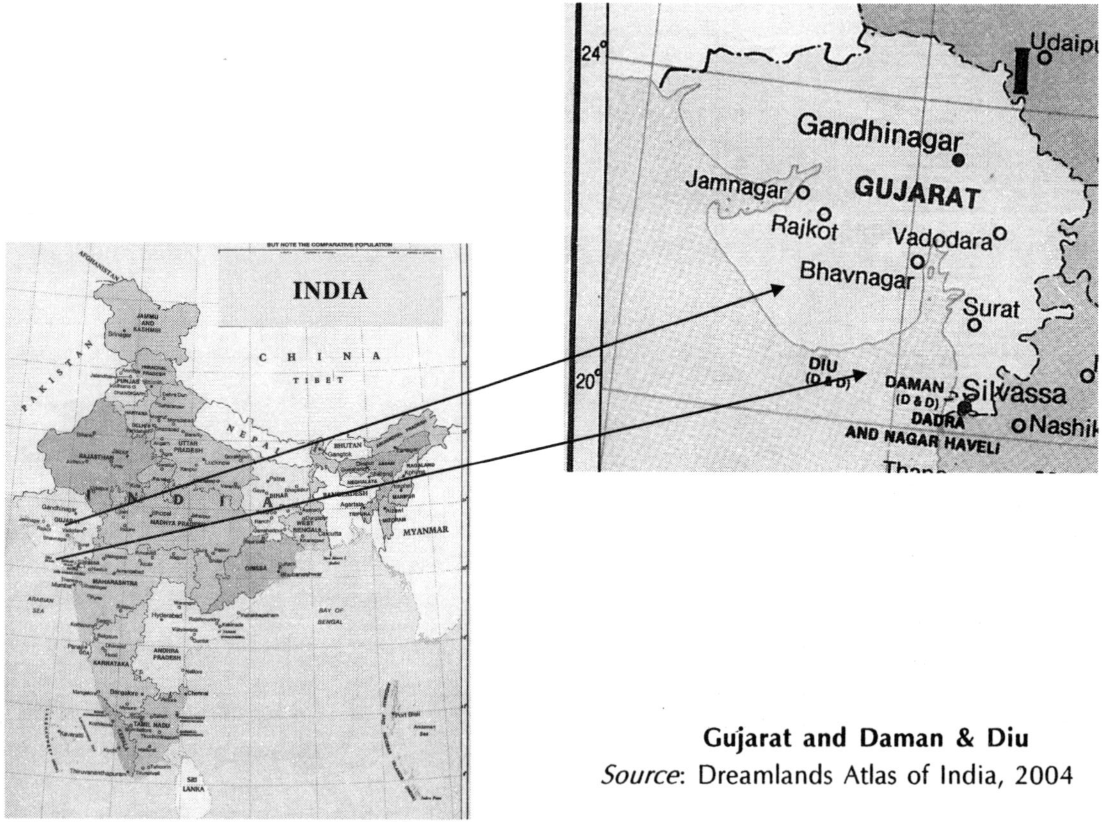


**Gujarat and Daman & Diu**

*Source*: Dreamlands Atlas of India, 2004

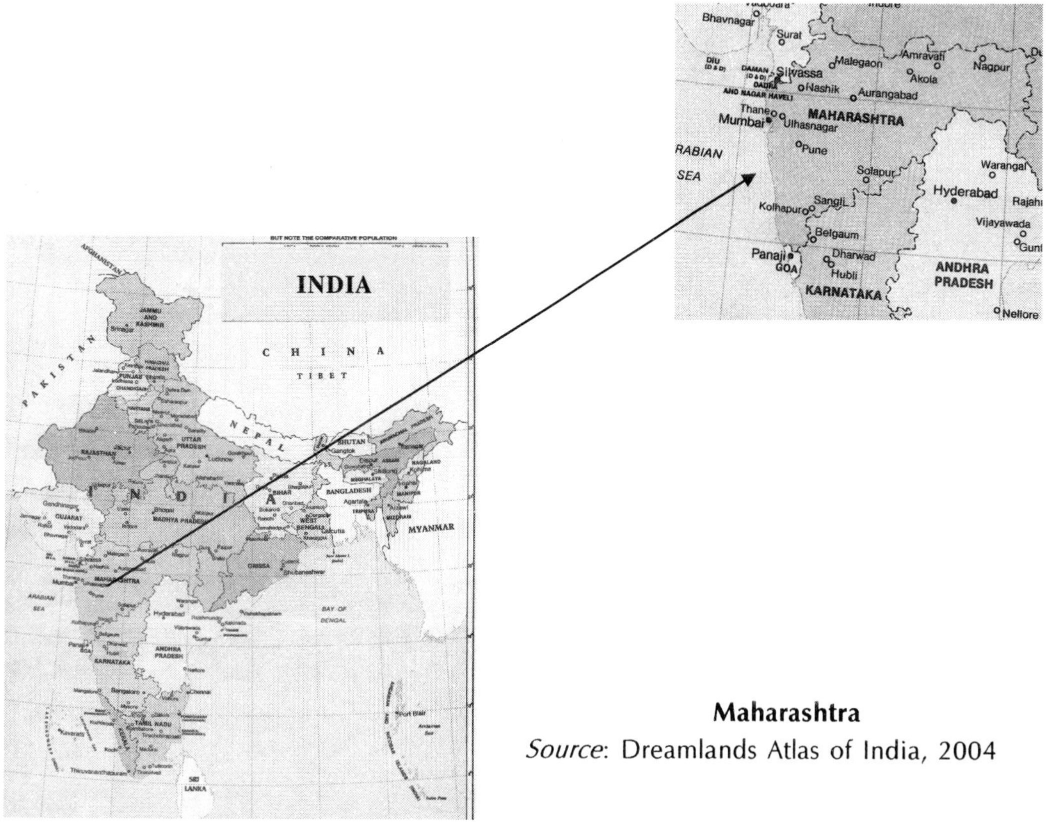


**Maharashtra**
*Source*: Dreamlands Atlas of India, 2004

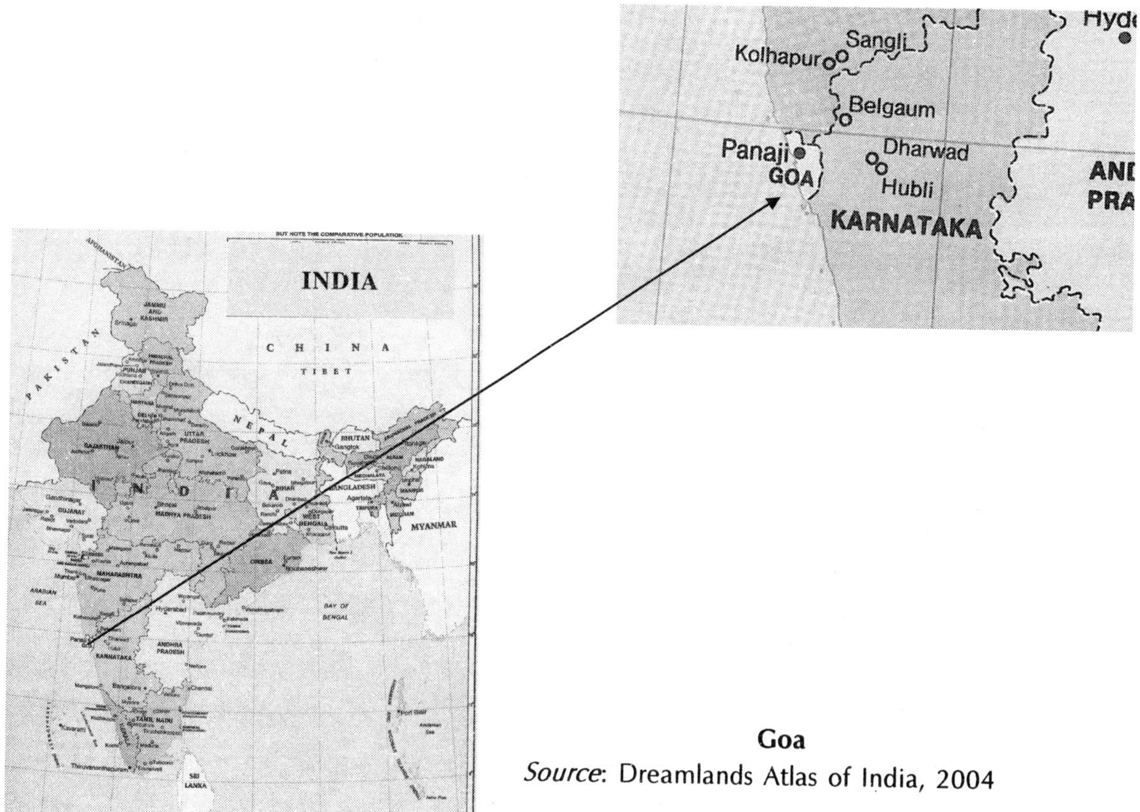


**Goa**

*Source*: Dreamlands Atlas of India, 2004

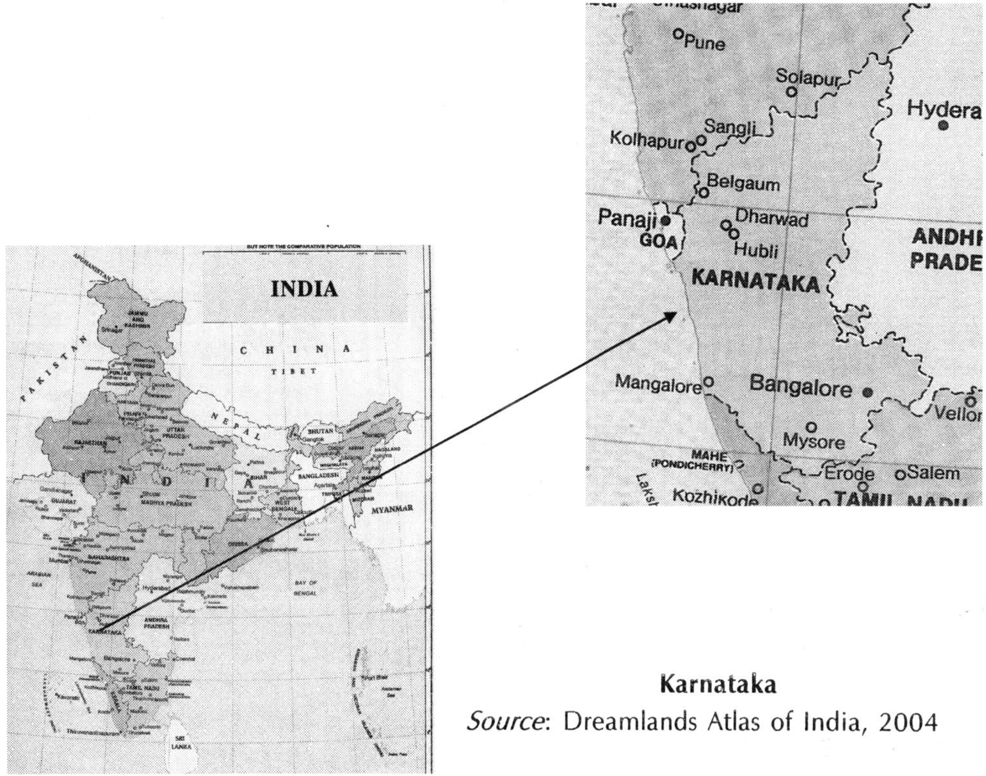


**Karnataka**

*Source*: Dreamlands Atlas of India, 2004

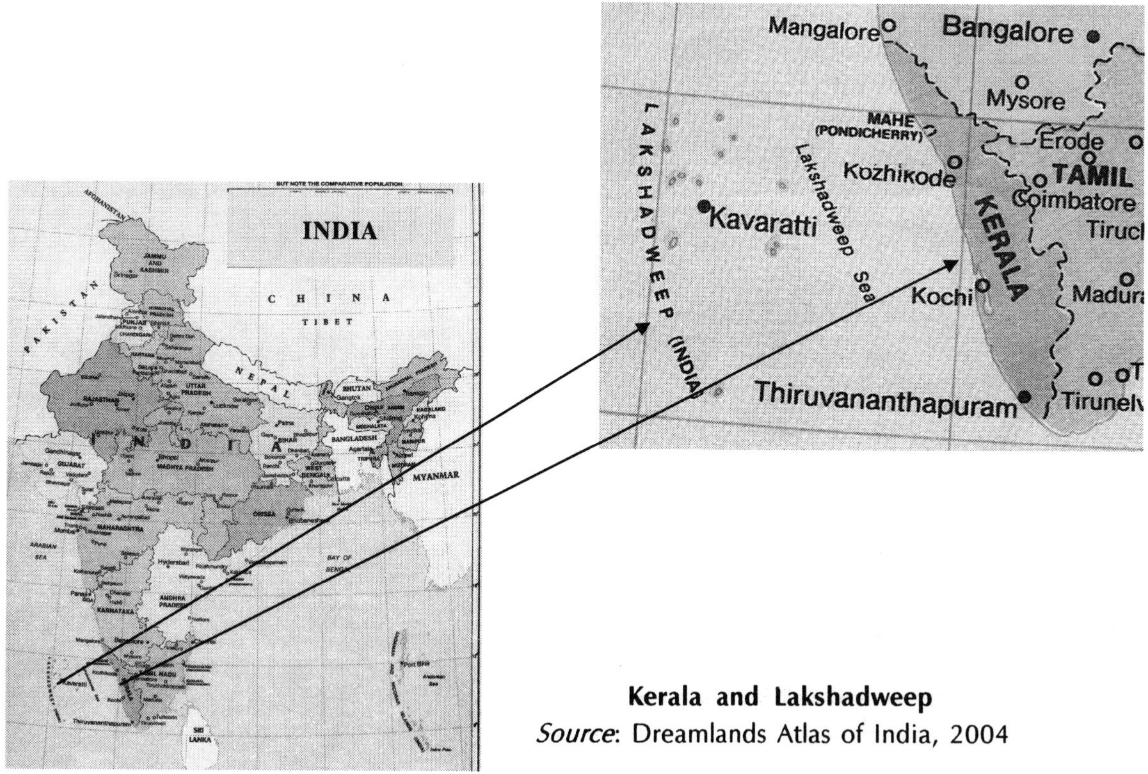


**Kerala and Lakshadweep**

*Source*: Dreamlands Atlas of India, 2004

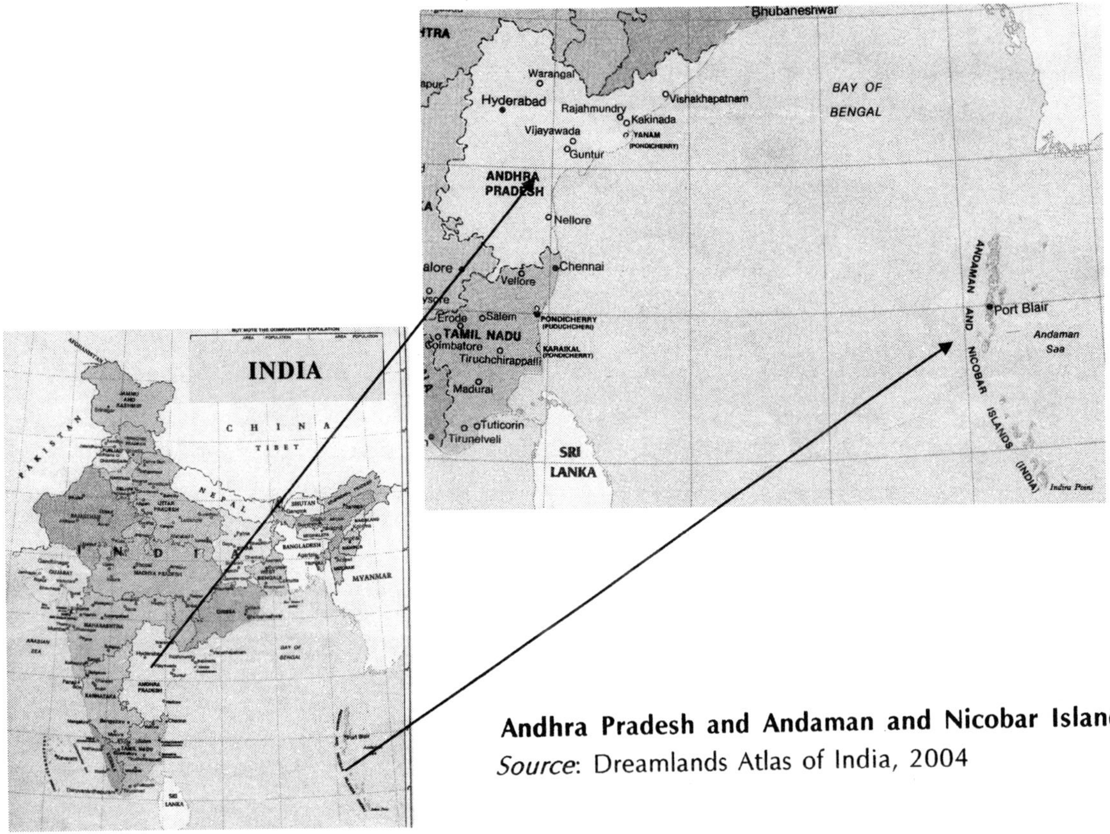


**Andhra Pradesh and Andaman and Nicobar Islands**

*Source*: Dreamlands Atlas of India, 2004

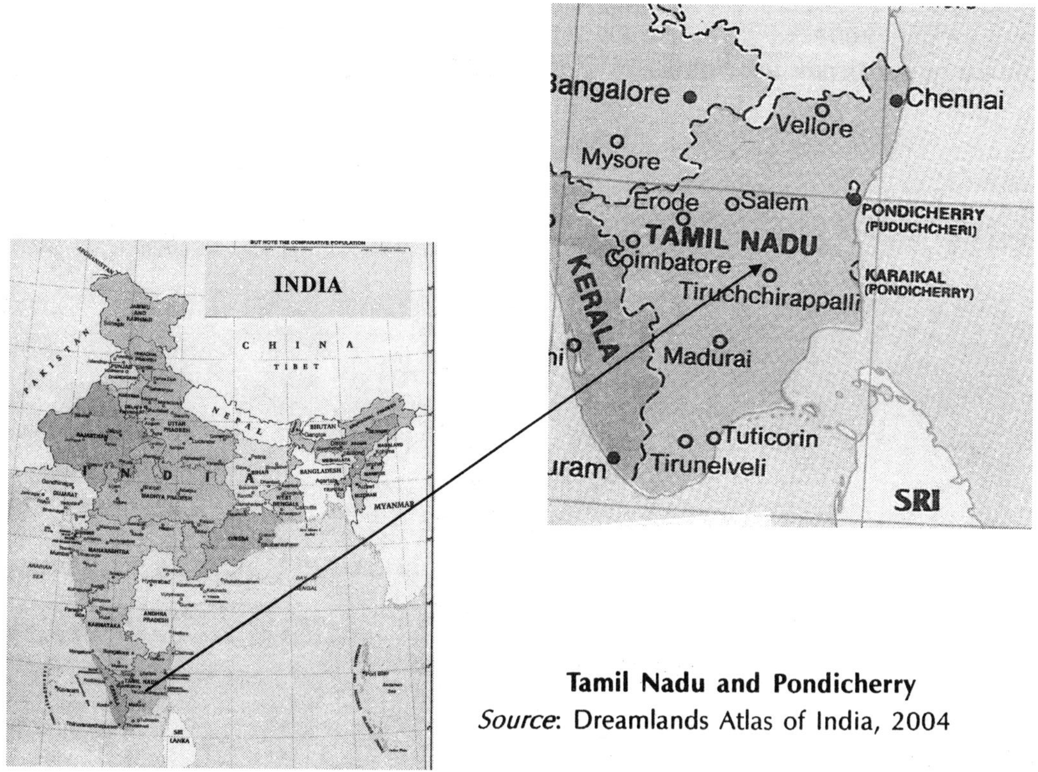


**Tamil Nadu and Pondicherry**
*Source*: Dreamlands Atlas of India, 2004

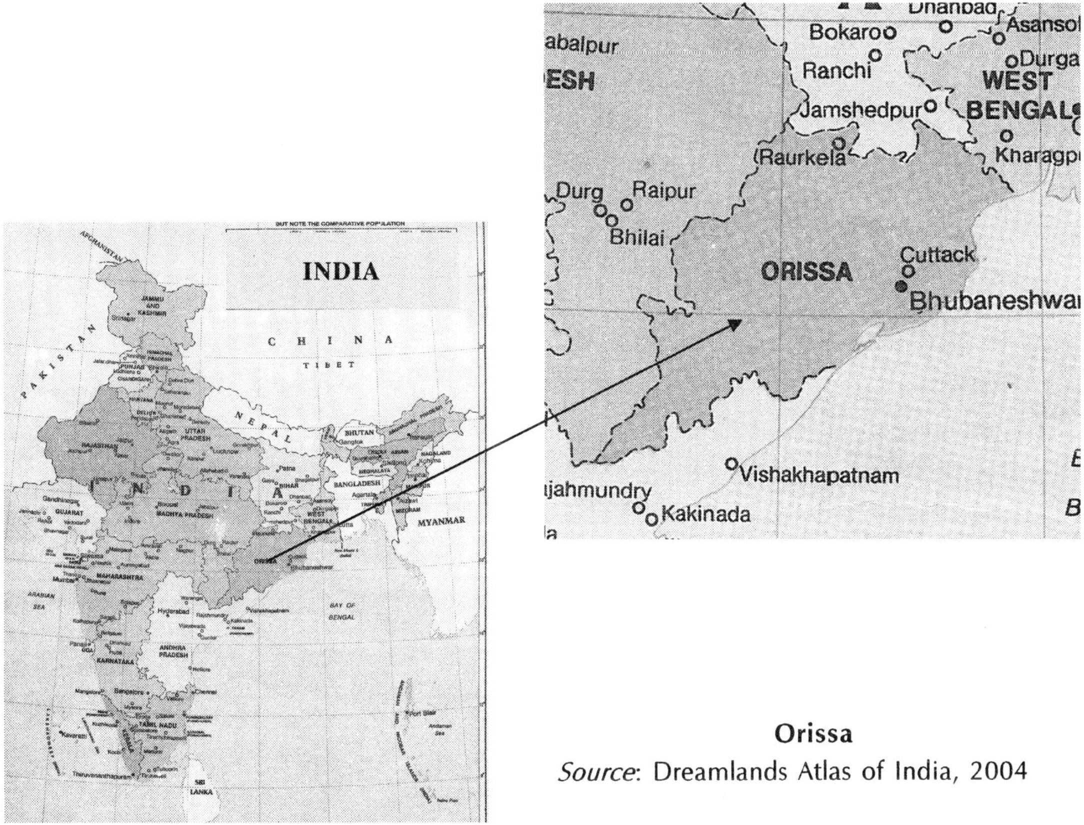


**Orissa**

*Source*: Dreamlands Atlas of India, 2004

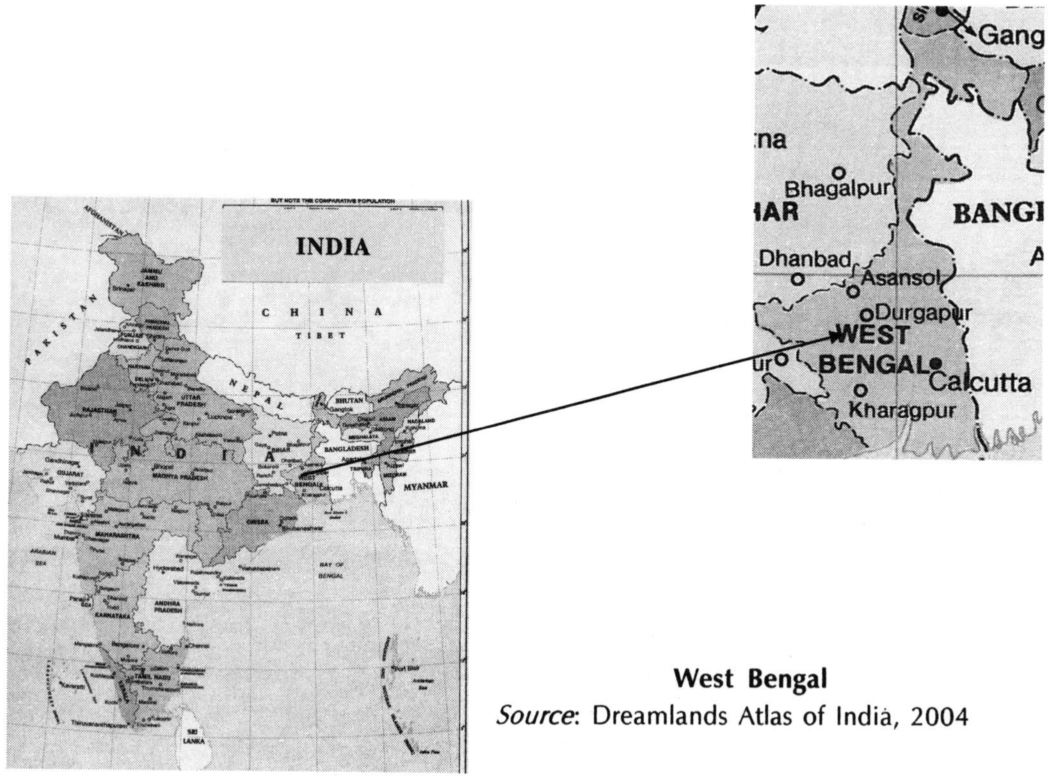


**West Bengal**

*Source*: Dreamlands Atlas of India, 2004

## India's Maritime Boundary Agreement

### India-Sri Lanka Agreement: On the Boundary in Historic Waters and Related Matters, 26 and 28 June 1974

**Table 1** India-Sri Lanka Maritime Bounday Coordinates-Palk Strait

| Point | Latitude North | Longitude East |
|---|---|---|
| 1 | 10° 05' | 80° 03' |
| 2 | 09° 57' | 79° 35' |
| 3 | 09° 40.15' | 79° 22.60' |
| 4 | 09° 21.80' | 79° 30.70' |
| 5 | 09° 13' | 79° 32' |
| 6 | 09° 06' | 79° 32' |

### India-Sri Lanka Agreement: On the Maritime Boundary Between the Two Countries in the Gulf of Mannar and the Bay of Bengal and Related Matters, 23 March 1976

**Table 2** India-Sri Lanka Maritime Bounday Coordinates-Gulf of Mannar

| Point | Latitude North | Longitude East |
|---|---|---|
| 1m | 9° 06'.0 | 79° 32'.0 |
| 2m | 09° 00'.0 | 79° 31'.3 |
| 3m | 08° 53'.8 | 79° 29'.3 |
| 4m | 08° 40'.0 | 79° 18'.2 |
| 5m | 08° 37'.2 | 79° 13'.0 |
| 6m | 08° 31'.2 | 79° 04'.7 |
| 7m | 08° 22'.2 | 78° 55'.4 |

| | | |
|---|---|---|
| 8m | 08° 12'.2 | 78° 53'.7 |
| 9m | 07° 35'.3 | 78° 45'.7 |
| 10m | 07° 21'.0 | 78° 38'.8 |
| 11m | 06° 30'.8 | 78° 12'.2 |
| 12m | 05° 53'.9 | 77° 50'.7 |
| 13m | 05° 00'.0 | 77° 10'.6 |

**Table 3** India-Sri Lanka Maritime Boundary coordinates - Bay of Bengal

| Point | Latitude North | Longitude East |
|---|---|---|
| 1 b | 10° 05'.0 | 80° 03'.0 |
| 1 ba | 10° 05'.8 | 80° 05'.0 |
| 1 bb | 10° 08'.4 | 80° 09'.5 |
| 2 b | 10° 33'.0 | 80° 46'.0 |
| 3 b | 10° 41'.7 | 81° 02.5 |
| 4 b | 11° 02'.7 | 81° 56'.0 |
| 5 b | 11° 16'.0 | 82° 24'.4 |
| 6 b | 11° 26'.6 | 83° 22'.0 |

**India-Sri Lanka-Maldives Agreement: Determination of the Tri-Junction Point Between the Three Countries in the Gulf of Mannar, 23, 24 and 31 July 1976**

**Table 4** India-Sri Lanka-Maldives Tri-Junction Coordination

| Point | Latitude North | Longitude East |
|---|---|---|
| T | 04° 47' 04" | 77° 01' 40" |

## India-Sri Lanka Supplementary Agreement: On the Extension of the Maritime Boundary Between the Two Countries in the Gulf of Mannar, 22 November 1976

The maritime boundary between India and Sri Lanka in the Gulf of Mannar beyond position 13 m, defined in the maritime boundary agreement of March 1976, upto the tri-junction point (Point T) defined in the trilateral agreement of July 1976 shall be arcs of Great Circles between the positions.

**Table 5** India-Sri Lanka Maritime Boundary Extension-Gulf of Mannar

| Point | Latitude North | Longitude East |
|---|---|---|
| 13m | 05° 00'.00 | 77° 10'.6 |
| T | 04° 47'.04 | 77° 01'.40 |

## India-Maldives Agreement: On the Maritime Boundary Between the Two Countries in the Arabian Sea and Related Matters, 28 December 1976

**Table 6** India-Maldives Maritime Boundary Coordinates-Arabian Sea

| Point | Latitude North | Longitude East |
|---|---|---|
| T | 04° 47' 04″ | 77° 01' 40″ |
| 1 | 04° 52' 15″ | 76° 56' 48″ |
| 2 | 05° 05' 35″ | 76° 43' 15″ |
| 3 | 05° 13' 56″ | 76° 36' 48″ |
| 4 | 06° 28' 14″ | 75° 41' 34″ |
| 5 | 06° 33' 21″ | 75° 38' 31″ |
| 6 | 06° 51' 06″ | 75° 25' 46″ |
| 7 | 07° 15' 27″ | 75° 16' 19″ |

| | | |
|---|---|---|
| 8 | 07° 24' 00″ | 75° 12' 06″ |
| 9 | 07° 25' 19″ | 75° 11' 18″ |
| 10 | 07° 51' 30″ | 74° 56' 09″ |
| 11 | 07° 48' 30″ | 74° 29' 45″ |
| 12 | 07° 41' 50″ | 73° 38' 34″ |
| 13 | 07° 39' 02″ | 73° 19' 38″ |
| 14 | 07° 40' 52″ | 73° 03' 23″ |
| 15 | 07° 42' 19″ | 72° 49' 30″ |
| 16 | 07° 42' 54″ | 72° 42' 26″ |
| 17 | 07° 49' 05″ | 72° 03' 45″ |
| 18 | 08° 05' 38″ | 72° 15' 08″ |
| 19 | 07° 57' 27″ | 69° 35' 45″ |

### India-Burma Agreement: Delimitation of the Maritime Boundary in the Andaman Sea, in the Coca Channel and in the Bay of Bengal, 23 December 1986

**Table 7** India-Burma Maritime Boundary coordination-Andaman Sea and Coca Channel

| Point | Latitude North | Longitude East |
|---|---|---|
| 1 | 09° 38' 00" | 95° 35' 25" |
| 2 | 09° 53' 14" | 95° 28' 00" |
| 3 | 10° 18' 42" | 95° 16' 02" |
| 4 | 10° 28' 00" | 95° 15' 58" |
| 5 | 10° 44' 53" | 95° 22' 00" |
| 6 | 11° 43' 17" | 95° 26' 00" |
| 7 | 12° 19' 43" | 95° 30' 00" |
| 8 | 12° 54' 07" | 95° 41' 00" |

| | | |
|---|---|---|
| 9 | 13° 48' 00" | 95° 02' 00" |
| 10 | 13° 48' 00" | 93° 50' 00" |
| 11 | 13° 34' 18" | 93° 40' 59" |
| 12 | 13° 49' 11" | 93° 08' 05" |
| 13 | 13° 57' 29" | 92° 54' 50" |
| 14 | 14° 00' 59" | 92° 50' 02" |

**Table 8** India-Burma Maritime boundary coordinates-Bay of Bengal

| Point | Latitude North | Longitude East |
|---|---|---|
| 14 | 14° 00' 59" | 92° 50' 02" |
| 15 | 14° 17' 42" | 92° 24' 17" |
| 16 | 15° 42' 50" | 90° 14' 01" |

## India-Burma-Thailand Agreement: Determination of the Tri-Junction Point Between the Three Countries in the Andaman Sea, 27 October 1993

**Table 9** India-Burma-Thiland Tri-Junction Coordinates

| Point | Latitude North | Longitude East |
|---|---|---|
| T | 09° 38' 00" | 95° 35' 25" |

## India-Thailand Agreement: Delimitation of Seabed Boundary Between the Two Countries in the Andaman Sea, 22 June 1978

**Table 10** India-Thailand boundary Coordinates-Andaman Sea

| Point | Latitude North | Longitude East |
|---|---|---|
| 1 | 07°48' 00" | 95° 32' 48" |
| 2 | 07° 57' 30" | 95° 41' 48" |
| 3 | 08° 09' 54" | 95° 39' 16" |

| | | |
|---|---|---|
| 4 | 08° 13' 47" | 95° 39' 11" |
| 5 | 08° 45' 11" | 95° 37' 42" |
| 6 | 08° 48' 04" | 95° 37' 40" |
| 7 | 09° 17' 18" | 95° 36' 31" |

**India-Thailand Agreement; Delimitation of Maritime Boundary Between the Two Countries in the Andaman Sea, 27 October 1993**

**Table 11** India-Thiland Maritime Boundary Coordinates-Adaman Sea

| Point | Latitude North | Longitude East |
|---|---|---|
| 7 | 09° 17' 18" | 95° 36' 31" |
| T | 09° 38' 00" | 95° 35' 25" |

**India-Indonesia Agreement: Determination of the Tri-Junction Point Between the Three Countries in the Adaman Sea, 22 October 1978**

**Table 12** India-Thailand-Indonesia Tri-junction coordinates-Adaman Sea

| Point | Latitude North | Longitude East |
|---|---|---|
| T | 07° 47' 00" | 95° 31' 48" |

**India-Indonesia Agreement: Delimitation of the Continental Shelf Boundary Between the Two Countries, 8 August 1974**

**Table 13** India-Indonesia Continental Shelf Boundary Coordinates-Great Nicobar and Sumatra

| Point | Latitude North | Longitude East |
|---|---|---|
| 1 | 06°38' 05" | 94° 38' 00" |
| 2 | 06 30' 00" | 94° 32' 04" |

| | | |
|---|---|---|
| 3 | 06° 16' 02" | 94° 24' 02" |
| 4 | 06° 00' 00" | 94° 10' 03" |

**India-Indonesia Agreement: Extension of the 1974 Continental Shelf Boundary Between the Two Countries, in the Adaman Sea and the Indian Ocean, 14 January 1977.**

**Table 14** Indonesia Maritime Boundary Coordinates-Andaman Sea

| Point | Latitude North | Longitude East |
|---|---|---|
| 1 | 06°38' 05" | 94° 38' 00" |
| K | 07° 02' 24" | 95° 55' 37" |
| N | 07° 40' 06" | 95° 25' 45" |
| O | 07° 46' 06" | 95° 31' 12" |

**Table 15** Indonesia Maritime Boundary Coordinates-Indian Ocean

| Point | Latitude North | Longitude East |
|---|---|---|
| 4 | 06°00' 00" | 94°10' 03" |
| R | 05° 25' 20" | 93° 41' 12" |
| S | 04° 27' 34" | 92° 51' 17" |
| T | 04° 18' 31" | 92° 43' 31" |
| U | 04° 01' 40" | 92° 23' 55" |

Appendix 4

# Beaches and World Heritage Cultural Sites along the Indian Coast

## Beaches Along the Indian Coast

### Ahmedpur Mandvi

Just 125 kms along the coastline from Chorwad lies this unusual beach resort designed as a traditional ethnic Saurashtrian village. Cottages modelled on rural Gujarati architecture look out onto a secluded beach, one of the state's chief centres for water sports.

### Andaman and Nicobar

On the east coast of India, the rich forested islands of Andaman and Nicobar lie scattered in the Bay of Bengal. There are 362 volcanic islands of which only 37 are inhabited. They form an idyllic archipelago of gleaming white sandy beaches, a crystal-clear turquoise sea teeming with fish, and picturesque coral reefs. The lush green islands have a colourful historical past, with strings of invasions by the French, Dutch, Japanese and British, setting off raging wars between the settlers and the native tribes. The Cellular Jail, where hundreds of Indian revolutionaries were imprisoned during the Indian freedom struggle, still stands. Descendents of these political prisoners and the local tribes of the area are the inhabitants of modern day Andaman and Nicobar.

The tropical rain forests that loom close to the seashore are home to unique species of birds, and to tribes that still haven't learned to use fire. Andaman is an experience quite unlike any other.

Sunbathe in the mellow sun as you sip from a fresh coconut. Then swim out into the waves where dolphins and many-hued fish will give you company. The clear waters of the Andamans are ideal for snorkelling and scuba diving. The best beaches are at Wandour, Corbyn's Cove, Jolly Buoy and Ross Island.

**Bordi**

This quiet uncluttered beach town, 145 kms from Mumbai, is a great weekend getaway. It lies just North of Mumbai, on the Gujarat-Maharashtra border. Quiet and uncluttered, Bordi is known for its long stretch of clean beaches, chickoo orchards and casurina trees. The beach is the main attraction in the town: the sand is fringed with a series of orchards and is a perfect place to de-stress, sun bathe, swim or just go for long walks. The really empty stretches are in the South towards Dahanu and towards the north in Umergaon. Unlike other beaches in Maharashtra which are silver, the beaches in Bordi are golden. Bordi has a strong Parsi influence and is a good place to see and enjoy their culture.

**Dahanu**

The 17 kms long coastline offers up these unspoilt beaches. Dahanu has a plethora of fruit orchards and is most famous for its chickoos. Udwada the most famous shrine of the Zoroastrians is accessible from Dahanu. The sacred fire in this splendid temple has been kept alive for almost a thousand years.

## Digha

The seven km long, flat, hard beach, dotted with casuarina plantations, is close to the border with Orissa and a five hour drive from Kolkata. Here the river Hooghly becomes indistinguishable from the Bay of Bengal.

## Diu

Diu is a Portuguese colony like Goa. An off-shore island on the western coast, off the Gulf of Cambay, this coast has limestone cliffs, rocky coves and sandy beaches, the best of which are at Nagoa. Nagoa Beach is one of the best beaches of India, at the Nagoa hamlet in the village of Burcharwada. This horse-shaped beach, which is a two kms stretch, is exceptionally beautiful and quiet.

A massive fort built by Portuguese dominates the skyline. Diu is connected to the mainland by a narrow channel on the north with no commercial exploitation or environmental degradation, it offers pristine golden beaches, palmgroves and monuments of yesteryears. Nagoa, Jallandhar, Gomatimata and Chakratirth beaches are some of the popular beaches.

For those wanting to do some exploring, the battlement of Div Fort, St Paul's and St Thomas churches, temples of Dwarka, Somnath, Palitana and Sansan Gir Sanctuary are perfect places to visit.

## Goa

Goa is a tiny speck of sun-drenched, palm-fringed, hillock-speckled, lush-green-field-dappled paradise, skirted by white-topped sprays of salty blue waves. But then, Goa is a lot of things. This little seaside state, with an identity that's a seamless blend of Latino influence and Indian tradition, was crackling enough to have been one of the millennium destinations of the world.

The essence of Goa lies in its marvellous expanses of palm-fringed beaches and azure-blue seas, all warmed by the sun and local hospitality. Goa is all about relaxed lifestyle, enlivened by the Goan love for music and dance, spiced up by its superb cuisine. Summers on the golden sands, winters in the warm waters, or soaking in the Goan rains - Goa is exhilarating round the year. The scenic splendor of Goa simply dazzles as nature bares her treasures, unfolding miles and miles of glorious vistas of rivers, ponds, wooded hills and valleys. Whitewashed churches and temples at strategic points heighten the effect.

There's more to Goa than sun, sand and natural beauty. The allure is quite distinct from the rest of India - its not just the familiar remnants of European colonialism or the picture book exoticism that makes it so accessible, its the prevalence of a form of social and political progressiveness that westerners feel they can relate to. Goans are friendly and happy-go-lucky. They are fond of the good things in life and are certainly not caught up in the rat race.

**Gokarna**

Locals believe that Gokarna derives its name from the legend in which Lord Shiva emerged from the ear of a cow. Literally meaning the 'cow's ear', this village is formed by the ear-shaped confluence of two rivers. Adventurous travellers must be prepared for a bit of cliff scrambling. Om beach, one of Gokarna's five famed beaches, takes the shape of an 'Om', a spiritual symbol. The other beaches, wedged between gigantic cliffs that protrude like delicate fingers into the sea, are Gokarna, Kudle, Half-moon and Paradise. The drive up the winding path that leads to Gokarna is a scenic delight with the Rocky Mountains and Western Ghats on one side and the Arabian Sea on the other. Accomodation is available at guesthouses run by local families.

### Gopalpur

On the east coast of Orissa, this quiet beach is ideal for boating and yachting. It is a surfer's delight and excellent for sailing. A golden beach fringed by sand dunes and ruins of an old jetty from where, in medieval times, sailors set out to Indonesia, make this an ideal place for a relaxing holiday. A perfect beach, fairly isolated and undisturbed by the day-trippers.

The hot springs of Taptapani are an hour's drive from here. It is known to be a splendid retreat for sea worshippers, located about 16-km from Berhampur. You can still see the crumbling walls and pillars of the jetty which are witness to its past glory of commercial activity.

With an increase in tourist trade in the late seventies, and the opening of luxury hotels, a slow revival began and today Gopalpur-On-Sea is one of the foremost beach resorts in India.

### Karwar

With gentle waves, miles of golden sand, a tranquil ambience and acres of emerald foliage, Karwar has all the makings of perfect holiday destination. The captivating landscape is ringed with rugged hill ranges, thick woods and mysteriously deep valleys. Devbagh is the most enchanting of the five islands along the Karwar coast. It is this paradise which inspired the great Indian writer, Rabindranath Tagore, to pen his first play. The Sadashivgad Hill Fort with a Durga Temple, the unique Octagonal Church, the 300-year old Venkatrama Temple with ochre paintings, and the Naganatha Temple where an anthill is worshipped, are all worth visiting.

### Kaup

Situated 12 km south of Udipi, on the coastal belt that passes through the West Coast National Highway, Kaup has a lovely beach, a ruined fort and an old 100 ft light house. The two temples of Goddess Mariamma in Kaup are famous. The Jain Basadis here are in ruins.

### Kihim

In the Alibagh district of Maharashtra, 120 kms from Mumbai, lie some of the most beautiful and secluded beaches on the Western coast of India.

Kihim is a beach near Mandawa, a tiny hamlet best known for its mango orchards and coconut palms. The picturesque Kihim beach is not just a beach-lover's delight with its clean sands and seclusion, it is a treat for any avid nature lover with rare flowers, uncommon species of butterflies, and a variety of birds. Long walks in the groves, trekking around the fort and spectacular sunsets make this beach truly beautiful.

### Kovalam

Golden sands by the Arabian Sea.

The sheltered coves, the picture perfect tropical beaches, the palm-fringed bays in secluded coconut groves, the surf shampooing the shores ... all these make Kovalam a beach-bummer's delight. Like Calangute, Anjuna, and Colva in Goa, Kovalam has shed its hippy idyll.

Sip organic juices while you watch the fishermen heave their heavy wooden boats into the sea and cast their massive nets. These traditional vellams and catamarans have been used for years. Be there when they bring their catch early in the morning, and you'll be able to strike a bargain for some fresh barracuda, sea bass, catfish, tiger prawns, crabs, sardine, tuna, seerfish, pomfret, or mullet that you can get grilled at any of the stalls on the beachfront.

During the day, sprawl on the white sand in the mellow glow of the winter sun and enjoy the tropical fruit: succulent ripe mangoes, papaya, grapes, coconut water, bananas and pineapple. Then settle down for another snooze.

**Lakshadweep**

Be warned. There are some things that are really hard to find in Lakshadweep. Like fast cars, shrinks, or tranquilizers. They do have all that water though! Bright and clear as liquid glass.

Expect lush coconut groves, tranquil lagoons and long stretches of white sun-drenched beaches where the only sounds are the crash of waves and the breeze blowing through the palm trees. In Lakshadweep, nature is unspoilt, undisturbed and serene. The only throngs you'll ever see are of the sandpipers on the shore. Watch the spectacular marine life (sharks, green turtles, barracudas, corals, oriental sweetlip fish, hawksbill), or sleep by the sea with the night sky as your ceiling ... therapy has never felt better.

Geographically similar to that other divers' haunt, Lakshadweep is like the Maldives without the crowds. Situated in the Arabian Sea, 400 kms off the coast of Kerala, this group of 36 coral islands and atolls can be reached by a twenty-hour sea journey from Kochi (formerly Cochin).

The five islands that are inhabited are Kavaratti, Kalpeni, Kadmat, Minicoy and Bangaram. They are ideal for fishing, yatching, diving, snorkelling, and deep sea fishing.

Only two islands, Bangaram and Kadmat, are open to non Indians. There are dive centres on both these islands.

### Malpe

About six kms from Udipi at the mouth of the Malpe river, is the natural harbour of Malpe, an important fishing centre that enriches Karnataka's coastline with its fabulous beach. The endless stretch of golden sand, graciously swaying palm trees, clear blue sky and gentle murmur of the sea, all set the perfect mood for an idyllic holiday. Don't miss out on the Balarama Temple. St. Mary's Island, another delightful getaway spot right across from Malpe, is only a boat ride away. The island is 300m long and 100m wide and has a few palm trees. The unique basalt rock formations here jut out of the Arabian Sea to break into startlingly perfect octagonal shapes.

### Mamallapuram

South of Chennai on the shores of Bay of Bengal, Mamallapuram was once a port city of the Pallava rulers. The temples and rock cut sculptures of that period create a unique blend of history and natural beauty. The monuments of Mamallapuram are excellent specimen of Dravidian temple architecture and Pallava art.

The art in the marvellous monuments with sculpted panels, caves, monolith rathas and temples lay emphasis on robust earthly beauties, imbibed with life. The sculptures are breathtakingly real and artistic. The Pallavas were followers of Jainism but the conversion of Mahendra Verman to Shaivism had drastic consequences on the future of Jainism and it also explains the Shiva and Vishnu temple at Mamallapuram.

The Shore temple is perhaps the most photographed monument in India after Taj Mahal. The temple is floodlit in the night and is a pure visual delight. The pleasure of watching the monument in light with cool breeze from the sea has no comparison. Mamallapuram attracts tourists from all over the globe to its monumental splendour and sunny beaches.

### Marawanthe

Take in the spectacular views at Marawanthe, a seaside town where the West Coast Highway cruises along with the Arabian Sea on one side, and the river Sauparnika against the picturesque Kodachardi Hills forms a backdrop on the other. Marawanthe wears the look of a fairyland at sunset when the sky turns crimson, and the golden rays of the sun are reflected in the sea as well as the river. Watersports promise an action-filled holiday.

### Marve-Manori-Gorai

To the north of Mumbai lie these three calm and pleasant beaches. Marve — an attractive, intriguing fishing village which provides breathtaking sights of sunset and sunrise from the low-lying hills.

Gorai and Manori, a little further away, though a trifle crowded with revellers, are popular for their wonderful all night beach parties. Manori is a sleepy beach near the Portuguese flavored fishing village. It is in a rural enviroment, on an island off Mumai's north-western shore, about 55 km from the city centre.

### Murudeshwar

Visit Murudeshwar for a unique beach experience. Rediscover your love for solitude by sitting at a vantage point on a hillock and watching the relentless waves crash against the rock. Murudeshwar has a Shiva Temple and the tallest Shiva statue in India.

### Pondicherry

A tiny town on the eastern coast of India, Pondicherry is a beachcomber's delight. Though more famous for its French connection (it was a former French colony), Pondicherry has some of the country's most spectacular beaches and endearing backwaters.

The sparkling sandy beaches are absolutely isolated and one can enjoy endless miles of beautiful blue waters in solitude. The backwaters offer interesting river cruises.

### Ullal

Make footprints on the sand at this secluded beach backed by the sensational sway of casuarinas trees. Situated on the south bank of the Netravati river, just eight kms from Mangalore, Ullal's claim to fame is the courageous Queen Abbakka, who in the early 1600's repulsed a Portuguese attack near the city, killing two naval commanders and 200 Portuguese seamen. The ruins of the area indicate that it was a kingdom ruled with pomp and splendour. Ullal is also reputed for the Durgah of Syed Mohammed Shereeful Madani, who is said to have come to Ullal from Madina, 400 years ago.

### Vengurla-Malvan

Vengurla, on the southern part of the Maharashtra coastline, boasts of a long stretch of shimmering sand. It also houses the famous Shri Devi Sateri temple and the Rameshwar temple. Nearby are the Vengurla rocks, also known as Burnt Islands. The Sindhudurg and Padamgad forts are housed in the old township of Malvan, a former trading centre. Today, Malvan houses salt pans and is famous for the China clay pottery and mouth-watering Malvan cuisine.

### Vijaydurg-Sindhudurg

Once-upon-a-time, these were naval bases. Both have splendid beaches. The Sindhudurg or Ocean fort spans over 48 acres. Within its premises are temples dedicated to Bhavani, Mahadeo, Jarimai, Mahapurush and Shivaji, the last being the only shrine of its kind in India.

### Vishakhapatnam

Legend has it that Vishakhapatnam derives its name from a temple deity, Visakha, the God of valour. A Hindu king, enamoured by the lavish locale, built a shore-temple devoted to the God in the 11th century, on his way to Benares. Over the years, the mighty sea eroded the standing edifice, but the name and the town have remained. Vishakhapatnam became popularly known as Vizag, and Waltair as well. Maharajas and rich rulers, seafarers and maritime warriors, priests, philosophers and even pirates have all left their mark on this beach paradise on the Coromandel Coast. At one time, Vizag formed a part of the magnificent Kalinga Empire, under the domain of Emperor Ashoka in 260 B.C. Subsequently, the region fell into the hands of the Andhra kings of Vengi and then to the Pallavas and the Cholas.

It was in the 15th century that Vishakhapatnam became a part of the powerful Vijayanagar Empire. Using the seaport to their advantage, the kingdom exported valuable arts, artifacts and artisans to far-off regions such as Cambodia, Thailand, Malaysia, Burma and Indonesia. With the advent of the Europeans, particularly the British, Vishakhapatnam was slowly transformed into a port town. After Independence, the town emerged as an industrial centre with a steel plant, an oil refinery and a fertilizer factory. It also has the country's largest ship building yard. One can visit any of these thriving industries with prior permission to get an overview of how large enterprises operate.

## World Heritage Cultural Sites along the Coast

### Old Goa

Gently-swaying palms, heavy with fruit; stretches of smooth, golden sand, disturbed only by the zigzag patterns left by sandcrabs and the rhythmic crashing of frothy waves. This is what lures tourists to Goa and few of them venture beyond the beaches. But take a drive through the less-popular interiors of Goa and experience its unique cultural heritage.

The impact of 450 years of Portuguese colonial rule is apparent in every aspect of Goan life - in the food and dress, in the houses painted in gay colours and in the joie de vivre of the people. In every village, the fresh lime-washed facade of a church stands out like a beacon in the deep green countryside.

The Portuguese explorer Alphonoso de Albuquerque captured Goa in 1510 and the Portuguese ruled the territory till its independence on 19 december 1961. The colony of Goa, with its epicentre at Goa Velha or Old Goa, became the capital of the vast eastern empire of the Portuguese, sharing the same civic privileges as Lisbon. It was often described as Goa Dourada or Golden Goa.

The early efforts of the Roman Catholic missionaries to introduce Christianity into Goa were rather half-hearted until the arrival in 1542 of the Jesuits, who were driven by the zeal of medieval crusaders. Francis Xavier, one of the founders of the Society of Jesus, better known as the Jesuits, rapidly became the patron saint of Goa.

The court in Lisbon instructed the civil administration in Goa to render maximum support to the church and huge amounts were diverted for the establishment of convents and monasteries. It is ironic that in the 17th century, even as Portuguese trade and commerce began dwindling, a grandiose effort was being made to erect more churches and cathedrals in Goa.

The churches in Old Goa aimed to overawe the local population into conversion and to impress upon them the superiority of the foreign religion. So the facades were made tall and lofty and the interiors were magnificent, with twisted Bernini columns, decorated pediments, profusely-carved gilt altars and colourful wall paintings and frescoes.

Locally available laterite was used in the construction of the churches while the trimmings were sometimes of basalt. Laterite being a very porous stone, the churches had to be plastered and finished with a lime white-wash. In fact, the colour white was so identified with churches that the local administration ruled that no house could be painted that colour.

By 1635, the following waves of epidemics, the seat of power moved from Old Goa to Panjim, bringing about its inevitable decline. Looking at the overgrown jungle that covers most of Old Goa, it is difficult to imagine that the city once had grand houses and crowded bazaars with elegant shops. All that remains are a dozen churches, convents and monasteries.

The best way to do justice to the great city of Old Goa, is to first visit the group of three big churches - the Basilica of Bom Jesus, the Cathedral and the Church and Convent of St Francis of Assisi. The latter houses the Archaeological Museum. Thereafter, visit the Chapel of St Catherine (1510) and the ruins of the Palace of the Inquisition, before taking a walk down the quay to view the remnants of a once bustling city. Stop briefly at the Vicerory's Arch that was rebuilt in 1599.

East of the Vicerory's Arch is the Church of St Cajetan and the Gate of the palace of Adil Shah. What was formerly Adil Shah's principal palace was used as the Viceroy's residence from 1554-1695.

To get the best hilltop view, climb the Holy Hill. Quite a few churches and convents are scattered over the hillside: the Church of Our Lady of the Rosary is one of the earliest churches built; the Royal Chapel of St Anthony (1543), the patron saint of Portugal; the Church and Monastery of St Augustine; the convent of St Monica and the Church and Convent of St John of God (1685). Climb down the hill and turn left till you hit the highway that takes you back to the Basilica.

**Ajanta Caves**

Way back in 1819, a party of British army officers on a tiger hunt in the forest of western Deccan, suddenly spotted their prey, on the far side of a loop in the Waghora river. High up on the horseshoe- shaped cliff, the hunting party saw the tiger, silhouetted against the carved facade of a cave.

On investigating, the officers discovered a series of carved caves, each more dramatic than the other. Hewn painstakingly as monsoon retreats or varshavasas for Buddhist monks, the cave complex was continuously lived in from 200 BC to about AD650. There are thirty caves, including some unfinished ones. Of the Ajanta caves, five are chaityas or prayer halls and the rest are viharas or monasteries.

The Ajanta caves resolve themselves into two phases, separated from each other by a good four hundred years. These architectural phases coincide with the two schools of Buddhist thought, the older Hinayana school where the

Buddha was represented only in symbols like the stupa, a set of footprints or a throne, and the later Mahayana sect which did not shy away from giving the Lord a human form.

Among the more prominent Hinayana caves are those numbered 9, 10 (both chaityas), 8, 12, 13 and 15 (all viharas). The sculpted figures in these caves are dressed and coiffed in a manner reminiscent of the stupas at Sanchi and Barhut, indicating that they date back to the 1$^{st}$ or 2nd century BC.

The Mahayana monasteries include caves 1, 2, 16 and 17, while the chaityas are in caves 19 and 26. The caves, incidentally, are not numbered chronologically but in terms of access from the entrance. A terrqaced path of modern construction connects the caves, but in ancients times, each cave was accessed from the riverfront by individual staircases.

The sculptures and paintings in the caves detail the Buddha's life as well as the lives of the Buddha in his previous births, as related in the allegorical Jataka tales. You will also find in the caves a sort of illuminated history of the times - court scenes, street scenes, cameos of domestic life and even animal and bird studies come alive on these unlit walls.

## Elephanta

A dark cave on a tiny island, in the middle of Mumbai harbour, houses one of the most imposing examples of early rock-out architecture. Although not quite as spectacular as the Ajanta or Ellora caves, the Elephanta cave, a 10-km boat ride from the Gateway of India in Mumbai, is well worth a visit.

The cave temple, dedicated to Shiva, was excavated sometime in the 8th century by the Rashtrakuta kings who ruled the area between AD 757-973.

The setting of the Elephanta cave temple was deemed symbolic as the sea represents samsara, the turbulent river of life, and the island was, thus, a place of physical and spiritual refuge. Today, it bears little resemblance to a spiritual retreat; the steps up from the jetty are linked with souvenir shops and soft drink stalls and, on the weekend, the island turns into a virtual carnival, with day-trippers from Mumbai coming over in large numbers.

The island, known as Gharapuri or the Fort Town, was christened Elephanta by the Portuguese, who captured it from the Sultan of Gujarat in AD 1535. They named it for its huge sculpted elephant, but treated it with scant concern, turning the pillared mandapa into a shooting gallery and letting the famous elephant fall to pieces. The British, who annexed the island in the 1770s, had the broken figure removed to the Victoria Gardens adjoining the Victoria & Albert Museum in Byculla in Mumbai.

The cave temple, situated some 75 metres above jetty level, closely follows the pattern of the Dumar Lena cave in Ellora. Under this style, an isolated shrine is contained within a group of pillared halls that are arranged on a cruciform plan and have entrances in the wings as well. This allowed light to infiltrate the darkest depth of the cave. At Elephanta, for instance, the main image of Shiva as Maheshwara is so skillfully placed in relation to the three entrances, that it receives just the amount of light necessary to make it look as though the Lord is emerging from eternal darkness.

This image, placed in a vestibule at the end farthest away from the entrance, is the focus of the entire temple. The cave is devoid of minor decorations, which only heightens the effect of the monumental sculpted panels depicting Shiva in myriad forms.

Step into the foyer of the cave and find a carving of Shiva as Nataraja on your right and as Lakulisa on your left. Created in the Buddhist mould, the sculpture shows Lakulisa, a 7th century priest who did much to reabsorb Buddhists into Hindusim, seated on a lotus, the symbol of enlightenment.

The garbhagriha has entrances at the four cardinal points. Giant dwarapalas and their gana attendants guard these doorways. The shrine itself has a metre-high linga.

At the four corners of the main mandapa are the famous wall panels showing Shiva in many moods. Across the width of the hall is a representation of kalayanasundaram, the marriage of Shiva with Parvati. A coy Parvati and a confident Shiva are surrounded by her father Himalaya, the moon-god Chandrama, Brahma and Vishnu.

Right across the mandapa is a scene from the domestic life of Shiva and Parvati. The divine couple are shown playing dice. Parvati has obviously lost the game and is sulking prettily while her husband tries to woo her back to the game.

On the wall across from the entrance is the cave's centrepiece, the triple-headed figure of Shiva as Maheshwara or Lord of the Universe.

Standing high at 5.45 metres, the Trimurti statue depicts the three aspects of Shiva as creator, preserver and destroyer. The head on the left is generally believed to be that of Shiva's life-giving shakti, Uma, while the one on the right shows him as Rudra-Bhairava, a fearful figure with snakes in his hair. The central face is the swarupa or true self of Shiva – calm, serene and with his right hand (now broken) raised in benediction.

The enclosures contain a carving of Shiva as Ardhanarishwara - in which he combines the female and the male aspects in his own self - and a panel depicting the descent of the heavenly river Ganga to earth. Here, Ganga is shown in the company of her two tributaries, the Yamuna and the Saraswati.

**Ellora Caves**

Nestled in the crook of the Charanadari hill in Deccan is a series of ancient temples and monasteries hewn out of the moutainside. Situated on the ancient north- south trade route or the dakshinapatha, the tiny mountain village of Verul - mutated today to Ellora -was a well- known stopover for traders, priests and pilgrims who plied the route to the western ports.

Beginning sometime in the 7th century, when the Chalukyas (AD 553 - 753) ruled the Deccan, these wayfarers decided to make their presence permanent. And excavation started on a number of Buddhist chaityas and viharas. The place found favour with missionaries of other faiths as well, and over the next five centuries, Hindus and Jains also built their temples in the rocks there.

Unlike the caves at Ajanta, the Ellora caves were never 'lost'. Largely because it lay on a more frequented route, Ellora remained in the public eye. In fact, Kailasa Temple remained a practising shrine until the 19th century. Several travellers to India including the 10th century Arab geographer Al Masudi and Niccolao Manucci in early 17th century mention the caves in their accounts.

There are 34 caves, of which 12 are Buddhist, 17 Hindu and 5 Jain. The caves all face west, so are best seen in the afternoon. The Buddhist caves are to your far right as you face the curve of the Charanadari Hill, then come the Hindu ones, and finally, the Jain cave temples to the far left.

Although not too far removed from the Ajanta caves in terms of both space and time, the chaityas and viharas of Ellora are architecturally and sculpturally different. Compared to the Ajanta paintings and sculptures, the Ellora representations are more earthly, drawing elements from the Vajrayana school of Buddhism which was permeated with primitive ideas of magic and mysticism. So, the dwarapalas that flank each doorway, the gigantic Boddhisattavas and their consorts have a robust earthiness about them.

In fact, it is architectural skill rather than sculptural aesthetics that Ellora is noted for. Buddhist Cave 12 or Tin Tala, for instance, has a rather plain edifice with unadorned pillars and the sculptured panels are only on the inner walls. But its historical value lies in the fact that human hands fashioned a three-storeyed building from solid rock with such painstaking skill that even the floors and the ceiling are smooth and levelled. Tin Tala cave is a commodious monastery-cum-chapel, with cells enough to house 40 monks. It dates to the Rashtrakuta period in the middle of the 8th century and, in fact, the third floor, which contains the most sculpted decoration, was being excavated even as the Hindus were carving the magnificent Kailasa Temple further along the rock face. The cruciform layout of the third storey in Cave 12 may also be the inspiration behind the Dumar Lena (Cave 29) and the Shiva cave at Elephanta.

The other Buddhist caves as well as the first few Hindu caves are fairly unremarkable and do not prepare you for the magnificence of Kailasa Temple or Cave 16 - the largest monolithic structure in the world. Believed to have been started by the Rashtrakuta king, Krishna I, its excavation must rank as an architectural wonder. Two great trenches some 90 metres long were dug into the hillside. They were connected at the deepest point by another trench 53 metres across. The temple was meant to appear as though rising from a vast courtyard at ground level.

The great b!ɔck of residual rock, rising 30 metres, was then carved into the three-storeyed vimana, the main mandapa, two giant dhwajasthambas or pillars, and four sub-shrines. Beginning at the top, the mass of rock was hewn into shape, and as each layer was shaped, the carvers began ornamenting the structure. Each layer was thus hewn and decorated completely before moving downward, thus eliminating the need for any scaffolding.

The temple is dedicated to Shiva and named for his mountain home in the Himalayas, the snow-peak Kailasa. The main shrine and the Nandi mandapa are built on a plinth, over 7.8 metres high, with its entire vertical surface carved with mythical animals and gargoyles.

This is flanked on either side by two free-standing pillars, soaring some 15.9 metres high. These gracefully proportioned pillars are believed to have once borne the trishul or trident of Shiva.

Two storeys of corridors have been carved into the mountain, ringing the temple on three sides. These corridors are studded with small alcoves, all containing a wealth of sculpted figures telling the tales of the great Hindu epics, the Mahabharata and the Ramayana. Among the narrative friezes is the descent of river Ganga, and one of Ravana shaking Mount Kailasa. The architectural style and intricate sculpture is similar to Virupaksha Temple at Pattadakal that had been completed a decade before.

A further 2 kms along the rock-face are the Jain caves, the most recent of the lot, having been excavcted between AD 800-1100. Of these the Chhota Kailasa (Cave 30) and the Indrasabha (Cave 32) are the most noteworthy. Chhota

Kailasa is a miniaturised version of the stupendous Hindu Kailasa Temple.

However, the masterpiece of the Jain caves is the two-storeyed Indrasabha temple. The doorway opens onto a courtyard containing a small shrine, but the temple itself is a large edifice attained by a high flight of steps and flanked by a huge dhwajsthamba and a statue of an elephant. The three-sides of the central quadrangle are carved over to produce a two-storeyed facade containing a series of shrines to the many Jain tirthankaras or saints.

What staggers one at Ellora is the realisation that all that beauty one beholds was fashioned by human hand, more than a millenium ago.

**Hampi - City of Victory**

Hills of bare rock rise beside the swift Tungabhadra river as it swirls and curves through a barren landscape strewn with giant granite boulders. In this daunting terrain, many centuries ago, rose a magnificent medieval city that rivalled the most famous cities of the world - the imperial Vijayanagar or 'the City of Victory'.

Once the Vijayanagar empire dominated the land south of the Tungabhadra river. Its capital city, of the same name, was envied for its rich bazaars, crowded temples and fabulous palaces. Merchants and ambassadors from faraway lands came to its royal court looking for trade and alliances.

In the 14th century when large parts of northern India were already under Muslim rule, this region was part of the Hindu kingdom of Kampili. In 1326, the army of the ruler of Delhi, Mohammed bin Tughlaq defeated and killed the king of Kampili. Among those taken prisoner were two brothers, Harihara and Bukha, both treasury officers of Kampili, who were forced to convert to Islam. Some years later, the Sultan sent the brothers back to govern the province. In 1336 they laid the foundation of an independent kingdom, denied any allegiance to the Tughlaqs and became Hindus once again.

They laid the foundation of the Sangama dynasty with its citadel in Vijayanagar. The original name of the city was probably Vidyanagar after the great Hindu sage, Vidyaranya.

The greatest monarch of Vijayanagar was Krishna Deva Raya who reigned from 1509 to 1529. Travellers from Arabia and Italy came to his court and he had cordial diplomatic relations with the Portuguese at Goa. A scholar and poet, he was an enlightened and secular king. Krishna Deva Raya built some of the finest palaces and temples in Vijayanagar.

Many travellers have chronicled the magnificence of Vijayanagar. The Portuguese traveller Fernao Nuniz wrote, "What I saw seemed as large as Rome and very beautiful to the sight" while the Arab Abdur Razzaq felt that the beauty of Vijayanagar was such "that the pupil of the eye has never seen such a place".

For two centuries, until its disastrous defeat in 1565 by the combined armies of Bijapur, Golconda and Ahmednagar, Vijayanagar dominated the region. Thereafter, the city was abandoned and occupied by invaders who robbed and pillaged it, massacring its people and systematically destroying its buildings. Vijayanagar was left desolate, its pavilions and temples standing forgotten among palm trees and rice fields. It would be found in the early years of the 20th century - an amazing medieval city frozen in time, its ruins telling stories in stone of kings and warriors, temple dancers, merchants.

Robert Sewell, the British civil servant who discovered the ruins of Vijayanagar, wrote of its tragic end, "Never perhaps in the history of the world has such havoc been wrought, and wrought suddenly, on so splendid a city".

Today the monuments of the imperial city lie within the villages of Hampi and Kamalapuram in Bellary district of Karnataka, 353 kms from the nearest airport at Bangalore. The monuments are spread over 26 square kms and include a citadel area, a temple area, bazaars, fortifications, river landings and gateways.

The sculpture and architecture of Vijayanagar are noted for the elegance of design and intricate carvings. The local stone, granite and a green chlorite, were easily available and used with great imagination in buildings and free-standing sculptures.

**Konark Worshipping the Sun God**

Legends say that Samba, the son of Lord Krishna, was afflicted by leprosy because of a curse by his father. After a penance of 12 years, Samba was cured by Surya, the Sun God, in whose honour he built this temple.

Dedicated to the divine charioteer, Surya, the Sun Temple is a magnificent example of ancient Orissan temple and architecture. Built in the 13th century AD, it was visualised as a chariot for the Sun God for his daily celestial journey. It was built in the image of the chariot with seven horses (seven days of the week) and 12 pairs of wheels (12 months). Only a small portion of the original massive temple, the entrance hall (39 m in height) the Dancing Hall and a ruined temple remain. The word Konark is derived from two word elements - KONA means Corner and ARK means the Sun. The temple is also called the Black Pagoda.

Every aspect of life is shown here, and the erotic imagery depicts the sublimation of human love manifested in countless forms. Scenes from court, civic life and war are also done in detail.

The entrance is reached by a broad flight of steps, flanked on either side by prancing horses, the whole representing the chariot, in which the Sun-God rides across the heavens. The court of the temple, was decorated with large free-standing sculptures of great strength and beauty. Now protected under the World Heritage List, the temple's interior was filled up in 1903 A.D., by the then British Lieutenant Governor of Bengal, to save it from deterioration.

**Pattadakal**

Drive through the northern part of Deccan plateau, past miles and miles of sunflower and cotton fields, and it seems that the countryside has changed little since ancient times when the area was known as Karnata Desa or the Land of the Black Earth.

Tucked away in the interior of a state today known as Karnataka, is a dramatic gorge between two sandstone hills. Here lies Badami, the heart of the Chalukyan kingdom that ruled the Deccan between the 4th and 8th centuries AD. Badami, along with the other Chalukyan settlements of Aihole and Pattadakal forms a triangular circuit whose architectural fame attracts visitors from India and abroad.

The Chalukyas emerged as a major power after shaking off the yoke of their overlord, the Kadambas, in 6th century. Under great kings like Kirtivarman and Pulakeshin II, the Chalukyan domain was considerably enlarged. Harshvardhana, the ruler of Kannauj and one of the greatest emperors of ancient India, tried to invade the Chalukyan kingdom in AD 641 but was strongly rebuffed by Pulakeshin II.

The high point of Chalukyan rule was undoubtedly the regin of Vikramaditya II (AD 733 -746), whose territorial conquets were matched only by his brillant architectural creations. The temples of Pattadakal, to this day, bear testimony to the vigour and creativity of the Chalukyas, who have earned themselves a place in history as discerning patrons of art and architecture.

Pattadakal, a corruption of Pattada-Kisuvolal meaning Stone of Coronation, was the temple town on the banks of the Malaprabha river where the Chalukyan kings came to be crowned. The site is known to have been inhabited since prehistoric times. Ptolemy, the famous geographer (c. AD 150) refers to the place as Petrigal in his writings.

The ten main temples here live up to the Chalukyan reputation for eclecticism. It was here that we see the blending of the northern Indian Nagara and the southern Indian Dravida styles of architecture. Situated on the trading crossroads of the subcontinent, the Pattadakal architects picked up both influences and effortlessly blended them.

Frequent wars with the Tamil dynasty of the Pallavas - inscriptions at Pattadakal refer to them as prakriti-amitra or natural enemies of the early Chalukyas - led to the percolation of architectural knowledge and sculptural finesse. It is often remarked that Kailasnatha Temple at Kanchipuram strongly influenced the Virupaksha Temple at Pattadakal.

In Pattadakal, which forms the last phase of Chalukyan temple-building, you can see the shift in style from the Nagara to the Dravida form of temple building. The earlier temples like Papanatha, Jambulingesvara, Kadasiddesvara and Kasinatha represent the Nagara style, whose most prominent marker is its tapering shikhara or spire. The three great Shaivite temples of Sangamesvara, Virupaksha and Mallikarjuna, which collectively represent the apogee of Chalukyan architecture, are in the Dravida style, as are Galaganatha, Sunmesvara and the Jain temple outside the complex.

**Brihadisvara**

The most enduring aspect of the four-century rule of the Cholas (AD 850- AD 1280) was the extensive temple-building they undertook, creating a sacred circuit of 108 Shiva temples in the Kaveri delta.

Under Rajakesari Rajaraja who came to the throne in AD 985, and his son Rajendra I, the Cholas expanded their territories to cover the entire peninsula. As they went further, conquering the Maldive Islands, Sri Lanka, parts of Malaysia, and moving upwards to touch the river Ganga, their kingdom prospered.

A devout Shiva bhakta, Rajaraja - as also his son - gave thanks to the Lord by erecting grand temples. Soon, the landscapes of Tamil Nadu was punctuated with lofty spires or shikharas and magnificent temple gateways or gopurams.

At the heart of the Chola power structure, in the wondrous city of Thanjavur, Rajaraja erected his magnum opus, the Rajarajesvaramudayar. It was built as a tribute to his patron deity Shiva and also in expiation for the bloodshed he had caused in numerous wars.

The temple was consecrated in AD 1010, on the 275th day of the 25th reignal year of Rajaraja's reign, and it lives on, with all rituals and festivals duly conducted. The only thing that has changed is its name: during the rule of the Nayakas, who succeeded the Cholas, it was called Periya Udayar Koil, whose Sanskritised version is Brihadisvara. Today the locals call it just Periya Koil or the Big Temple.

Work on Brihadisvara began in AD 1003. The area around Thanjavur is fertile flatlands. The nearest rocky areas are around Thiruchirapalli, many miles away, from where the granite for the massive temple was probably quarried.

Slowly, the temple rose to tower over the countryside. Seven years later, the shikhara was ready, awaiting only the uttamavimana. Legend has it that a ramp of packed earth was constructed, beginning 6.4 kms away in the village of Sarapallam. The incline spanned the distance to reach the temple and elephants pulled the 81-tonne granite block mounted on logs to the top of the shikhara.

The two elaborately carved gopurams, widely separated from each other, lead the devotee to the huge 152 metres by 76 metres inner courtyard. Just ahead stands the monolithic granite statue of Nandi, Shiva's vehicle, ensconced under a painted canopy of the later Nayaka period.

The courtyard itself is encircled by a massive granite wall, which has 1008 Nandi statues on it. There are cloisters on three sides of this vast courtyard and the ones to the left house 108 Shiva lingas of different shapes and sizes.

Beyond is the central shrine, whose garbhagriha enshrines a massive 3.6 metre-high linga, striking in its simplicity. The huge black granite linga is also called the adavallan or One-who-dances-well.

The garbhagriha has a sandhara nali or circumambultory path between its inner and outer walls, allowing devotees to circle the shrine in a clockwise direction.

The passage round the garbhagriha is closed to the public and special permission from the Archaeological Survey of India is needed to enter it to view the few original Chola murals that survive. Unfortunately, most were painted over by the later rulers. Worth viewing is a line drawing showing Rajaraja and his mentor, the Shaivite saint Karuvur Devar.

There is another circumambulatory gallery on the first floor which is popularly called the Bharatnatyam Gallery because it contains statues of Shiva in the various dance poses described in the ancient dance treatise, the Natyashastra. Some 108 figures were planned, but only 79 were completed - in fact the 80th figure is left half-done -because the then king, Rajendra I, acquired a new centre of attention, the other Brihadisvara temple in his new capital Gangaikondacholapuram.

The Srivimana - the greatest attraction of the Thanjavur temple rises to a height of 66.8 metres from the base and is divided into 13 talas or storeys. The square chamber of the garbhagriha gives way to an octagonal hollow half-way up the spire for maximum load leverage. It is crowned by an 81-tonne block of granite called the uttamavimana, on which rests a gold-covered kalasha or finial, 3.6 metres high.

What makes this vimana unique is the almost microscopic adherence to measurements - and this in an age when precision tools were unknown. The viman is exactly eight times the width of the garbhagriha so that the load could be properly distributed. And the main Shiva linga, Nandi and the uttamavimana are all exactly 3.6 metres high.

**Mamallapuram**

Straddling the mouth of the Palar river, the sleepy town of Mamallapuram served the Pallava dynasty (AD 600-900) as its most important port on the Coromandel coast. It was from here that ships laden with spices and silks sailed across the Bay of Bengal to the islands of Java, Sumatra and to Cambodia.

Little wonder, then, that the Pallava kings chose this town to record their might in stone. The amazing pavilions and temples on the edge of the sea have withstood fourteen centuries to buffeting by the relentless elements, to be hailed as prototypes of Dravidian architecture.

Today, Mamallapuram is a quiet hamlet in the district of Chengalpet in Tamil Nadu. Also known as Mahabalipuram (legend has it that Lord Vishnu vanquished the giant Mahabali here), Mallapuram and Mahamalaipuram, it is 58 kms from Chennai and 72 kms from Pondicherry.

Even today, the town resounds to the sculptor's hammer. Encouraged by the government, the local stonecutters are continuing with a craft that first flourished here fifteen hundred year ago. In fact, the government has also set up a College of Sculpture here.

The Pallavas were the first major Tamil dynasty that ruled the region that is now Tamil Nadu between the 6th and 9th centurty AD. The area was then called Tondainadu.

The greatest Pallava king was Narasimhavarman (AD 640-668), fondly known as mamalla or little wrestler, who transformed a little seaside village into a bustling port and gave it its name.

The temples of Mamallapuram, built largely during the reigns of Narasimhavarman and his successor Rajasimhavarman, showcases the movement from rock-cut architecture to structural building. The mandapas or pavilions and the rathas or shrines shaped as temple chariots are hewn from the granite rock face, while the famed Shore Temple, erected half a century later, is built from dressed stone.

What makes Mamallapuram so culturally resonant are the influences it absorbs and disseminates. All but one of the rathas from the first phase of Pallava architecture are modelled on the Buddhist viharas or monasteries and chaitya halls with several cells arranged around a courtyard. Art historian Percy Brown, in fact, traces the possible roots of the Pallavan mandapas to the similar rock-cut caves of Ajanta and Ellora. Referring to Narasimhavarman's victory in AD 642 over the Chalukyan king Pulakesin II, Brown says the Pallavan king may have brought the sculptors and artisans back to Kanchi and Mamallapuram as 'spoils of war'. When the Chalukyans regained their kingdom, these workmen returned bearing memories of their work in the south with them. The similarities between Arjuna's Penance and Cave XXIV at Ajanta are particularly striking.

Some of Mamallapuram's other indigenous motifs, like the lion pilasters, the profuse decorations and precise figure sculptures and the nascent gopuram or gateway, in turn became leitmotifs of the southern style of temple building. Mamallapuram's influence can also be seen further afield in the Khmer sculptures of Angkor Thom and Angkor Vat in Cambodia and in the bas-reliefs at the Borobudur temple in Indonesia.

Of the secular architecture at Mamallapuram, the most fascinating is its elaborate water system. Little, however, remains of the non-religious buildings indicating that secular structures were probably made from less durable materials like brick and wood.

Source: Reproduced from Incredible India.Org
Website: http://www.tourismofindia.com/hibea/beaches.htm and http://www.tourismofindia.com/hiwhh/worldheritagehome.htm

Courtesy: Department of Tourism, Ministry of Tourism and Culture, Government of India 2002.

# Bibliography

## Books


Agardy, T S, *Marine Protected Areas and Ocean Conservation* (London: Academic Press Limited, 1997).

Alford, J, *Sea Power and Influence: Old Issues and New Challenges* (Hampshire: Gower Publishing, 1980).

Bateman, S and D Sherwood, *Australia's Maritime Bridge into Asia* (Australia: Allen & Unwin Pvt Ltd, 1995).

Beatley, T, D J Brower, and A K Schwab, *An Introduction to Coastal Zone Management* (Washington DC: Island Press, 1994).

Blake, G, *Maritime Boundaries and Ocean Resources* (London: Groom Helm, 1987).

Borgese, E M, *Ocean YearBook 13* (Chicago: University of Chicago Press, 1998).

Braun, D, *The Indian Ocean: Region of Conflict or Zone of Peace* (New Delhi: Oxford University Press, 1983).

Brown, B E, *Integrated Coastal Management of South Asia* (New Castle upon Tyne: University of New Castle, 1997).

Chandra, S, *The Indian Ocean Explorations in History: Commerce and Politics* (New Delhi: Sage Publications, 1987).

Chandra, S, Arunachalam, B and Suryanarayan, V, *The Indian Ocean and its Islands: Strategic, Scientific and Historical Perspectives* (New Delhi: Sage Publications, 1993).

Child, J, Organisation: *A Guide to Problems and Practice* (2nd edition, London: Paulchapman Publishing limited, 1988).

Childe, G, *What Happened in History?* (Reprint, Middlesex: Penguin Books, 1969).

Chowdhury, S, *Management 21C: Someday We'll All Manage This Way* (London: Pearson Education Ltd, 2000).

Cicin-Sain, B and Knecht, R W, *Integrated Coastal and Ocean Management* (Washington D C: Island Press, 1998).

Clark, J R, Coastal Seas: *The Conservation Challenge* (USA: Blackwell Science Ltd, 1998).

Coltrell, N J and Associates, *Sea Power and Strategy in the Indian Ocean* (United Kingdom: Sage Publications, 1981).

Couper, A, *The Times Atlas of the Oceans*. 1st edition (London: Times Books Ltd, 1983)

Davenport, T and Prusak, L, *Working Knowledge: How Organisations Manage What They Know* (Boston: Harvard Business School Press, 1998).

Davidson, M, *The Transformation of Management* (Hampshire: McMillan Business, 1995).

Drucker, P, *Management Challenges for the 21st Century* (Oxford: Butterworth & Heinemann, 1999).

Eden, C and Huxham, C, "Action research for the study of organisations" in Clegg, C, & Hardy, C, *Studying Organisation Theory and Method* (London: Sage Publications, 1999).

Edward d' Cruz, S J, *A Survey of World Civilisations* (Mumbai: Lalvani publishing, 1970).

Elkington, J, *Cannibals With Forks: The Triple Bottom Line of 21st Century Business* (Oxford: Capstone, 1997).

Evans, D R, Hearn, M T, Uhlemann, M R and Ivey, A E, *Essential Interviewing* (3rd edition, California: Brooks/Cole Publishing company, 1989).

Fabbri, P, *Ocean Management in Global Change* (London: Elsevier applied science, 1992).

Forbes, V L, *The Maritime Boundaries of the Indian Ocean Region* (Singapore: Singapore University Press, 1995).

Frankfort-Nachmias, C and Nachmias, D, *Research Methods in the Social Sciences* (5th edition, London: St Martin Press, 1996).

Friedman, N, *Sea Power as Strategy: Navies and National Interests* (Annapolis: US Naval Institute Press, 2001).

Ginther, K, Denters, E and Waart, P J I M, *Sustainable Development and Good Governance* (Netherlands: Martinus Nijhoff Publishers, 1995).

Glasson, T, Therivel, R and Chadwick, A, *Introduction to Environmental Impact Assessment* (4th edition, London: UCL Press Limited, 1996).

Gray, C S and Sloan, G, *Geopolitics: Geography and Strategy* (London: Frank Cass, 1999).

Gray, C S and Barnett, R W, *Sea Power and Strategy* (Annapolis: US Naval Institute Press, 1989).

Griffiths, M and 'O' Callaghan, T, *International Relations: The Key Concepts* (London: Routledge, 2002).

Grove, E, *The Future of Sea Power* (London: Routledge, 1990).

Gubbay, S, *Coastal and Sea Use Management* (Gloucester: Marine Conservation Society, 1989).

Hamton, D R, *Modern Management: Idea and Issues* (2nd edition, New Delhi: Prentice Hall, 1979).

Hill, J R, *Maritime Strategy for Medium Powers* (London: Croom Helm Ltd, 1986).

Kaplan,R S and Norton, D P, *The Strategy Focussed Organization: How the Balanced Scorecard Companies Thrive in the New Business Environment* (Boston: Harvard Business School Press, 2001).

Kay, R and Alder, J, *Coastal Planning and Management* (London: Routledge, 1999).

Kennedy, P, *The Rise and Fall of British Naval Mastery* (London: Penguin Books, 1976).

Kennedy, P, *The Rise and Fall of Great Powers* (New York: Random House, 1987).

Kurian, G T, *World Encyclopaedia of Parliaments and Legislatures,* Volume 1 (London: Fitzroy Dearborn Publishers, 1998).

Laffin, J, *Brassey's Battles - 3,500 Years of Conflict* Campaigns and wars from A-Z (London: Brassey's Defence Publishers, 1986).

Laurd, E, *The Control of the Seabed: A New International Issue* (London: Mayfair, 1974).

Lee A Kimball, L A, *International Ocean Governance Using International Law and Organizations to Manage Marine Resources Sustainably* (Switzerland: IUCN, 2001).

Miles, E L, "Future Challenges in Ocean Management: Towards Integrated National Ocean Policy," in Fabbri, P, *Ocean Management in Global Change* (London: Elsevier Applied Science, 1992).

Miller, A, *Strategic Management* (3rd edition, Boston: Irwin/McGraw Hill, 1998).

Miller, D, "Configurations of Strategy and Structure: Towards a Synthesis," in Segal-Horn, S., *The Strategy Reader* (Oxford: Blackwell Publishers Limited, 1998).

Mintberg, H, and Waters, J A, "Of Strategies, Deliberate and Emergent," in Segal-Horn, S, *The Strategy Reader* (Oxford: Blackwell Publishers Limited, 1998).

Mintzberg, H, and Quinn, J B, *The Strategy Process: Concepts, Contexts, Cases* (3rd Edition, London: Prentice Hall, 1998).

Modelski, G and Thompson, W R, *Sea Power in Global Politics, 1494-1993* (Seattle: University of Washington, 1988).

Ostroff, F, *The Horizontal Organisation* (Oxford: Oxford University Press, 1999).

Parry, J H, *The Age of Renaissance - Discovery, Exploration and Settlement 1450 to 1650* (London; Weidenfeld & Nicolism, 1963).

Prescott, J R V, *The Maritime Political Boundaries of the World* (London Methuen & Co Ltd, 1985).

Probst, G, Raub, S and Rombahardt, K, *Managing Knowledge: Building Blocks of Success* (New York: John Wiley & Sons Ltd, 2000).

Qasim, S Z & Roonwal, G S, *India's Exclusive Economic Zone: Resources, Exploitation, Management,* 1st Edition, (New Delhi: Omega Scientific Publishers, 1996).

Qasim, S Z & Roonwal, G S, *Living Resources of India's Exclusive Economic Zone* (New Delhi: Omega Scientific Publishers, 1998).

Ramachandran, S, "Coastal Zone Management in India- Problems, Practice and Requirements," in Salomons, W, Turner, R K, and de Lacuda, L D, *Perspectives on Integrated Coastal Zone Management* (New York: Springer-Verlaz Berlin Heidelberg, 1999).

Saunders, M N K, Lewis, P & Thornhill, A, *Research Methods for Business Students* (2nd edition, Essex: Pearson Education Limited, 2000).

Sawhney, M and Zabin, J, *Seven Steps to Nirvana: Strategic Insights into e-Business Transformation* (New Delhi: Tata McGraw-Hill, 2001).

Segal-Horn, S, *The Strategy Reader* (Oxford: Blackwell Publishers Limited 1998).

Sen, A, *Development as Freedom* (New York: Oxford University Press, 1999).

Simith, H D, *The Development of Integrated Sea-Use Management* (London: Routledge, 1991).

Smith, H D, *Advances in the Science and Technology of Ocean Management* (London: Routledge, 1992).

Starr, C G, *The Influence of Sea Power on Ancient History* (New York: Oxford University Press, 1989).

Taussik, J and Mitchell, J, *Partnerships in Coastal Zone Management* (Cardigan: Samra Publishing Limited, 1996).

Thakur, R and Newman, E, *New Millennium, New Perspectives: The UN, Security and Governance* (Japan: UN Press, 2000).

Timothy, B, Brower, D J, & Schwab, A K, *An Introduction to Coastal Zone Management* (Washington DC: Island Press, 1994).

Vallejo, S M A, "Integrated Marine Policies: Goals and Constraints," in Fabbri, P, *Ocean Management in Global Change* (London: Elsevier Applied Science, 1992).

Vogler, J, *The Global Commons* (New York: John Wiley and Sons, 1995).

## Journals

Abrahamson, E, "Change Without Pain", *Harvard Business Review* (Jul-Aug 2000).

Alphen, J V, "The Voordelta Integrated Policy Plan: Administrative Aspects of Coastal Zone Management in the Netherlands", *Ocean & Coastal Management,* Vol 26, No 2 (1995).

Ancona, D, Bresman, H and Kaenfee, K, "The Comparative Aadvantage of X-teams", *MIT Sloan Management Review,* Vol. 43, No. 3 (Spring 2002).

Bernard Dyer, B and Millard B, "A Generic Framework for Value Management of Environment Data in the Context of Integrated Coastal Zone Management", *Ocean & Coastal Management,* Vol 45 (2002).

Borgese, E M, "The Economics of the Common Heritage", *Ocean & Coastal Management,* Vol. 43 (2000).

Bouchikhi, H and Kimberly, R, "Escaping the Identity Trap", *MIT Sloan Management Review,* Vol. 43, No. 4 (Summer 2002).

Burbridge, P and Humphrey, S, "On the Integration of Science and Management in Coastal Management Research", *Journal of Coastal Conservation*, Vol. 5, Issue 2 (1999).

Burbridge, P R, "A Generic Framework for Measuring Success in Integrated Coastal Management", *Ocean & Coastal Management*, Vol 37, No 2 (1997).

Christie, P and White, A T, "Trends in Development of Coastal Area Management in Tropical Countries: From Central to Community Orientation", *Coastal Management*, No 25 (1997).

Cicin-Sain, B, "Sustainable Development and Integrated Coastal Management", *Ocean & Coastal Management*, Vol 21, No 1-3 (1993).

Clark, J R, "Coastal Zone Management for the New Century", *Ocean & Coastal Management*, Vol 37, No 2 (1997).

Collins, J C and Porras, J I, "Building Your Company's Vision', *Harvard Business Review*, (Sep-Oct 1996).

Dahl, C, "Integrated Coastal Resources Management and Community Participation in a Small Island Setting", *Ocean & Coastal Management*, Vol 36, No 1-3 (1997).

David Pinder, D, "Offshore Oil and Gas: Global Resource Knowledge and Technological Change", *Ocean & Coastal Management*, Vol 44 (2001).

Davos, C A, "Sustainable Co-operation as the Challenge for a New Coastal Management Paradigm", *Journal of Coastal Conservation*, Vol 5, Issue 2 (1999).

Dronkers, J and de Vries, I, "Integrated Coastal Management: The Challenge of Transdisciplinarity", *Journal of Coastal Conservation*, Vol 5, Issue 2. (1999).

Ducrotoy, J P and Pullen, S, "Integrated Coastal Zone Management: Commitments and Developments from an International, European, and United Kingdom Perspective", *Ocean & Coastal Management*, Vol. 42 (1999).

Ellsworth, J P, Lawrence, P H and Glover, E A, "Canada's Atlantic Coastal Action Program: A Community Based Approach to Collective Governance", *Ocean & Coastal Management*, Vol 36, No 1-3 (1997).

Freidheim, R L, "Ocean Governance at the Millennium: Where We Have Been - Where We Should Go", *Ocean & Coastal Management*, Vol. 42, No. 9 (1999).

Friedheim, R L, "Ocean Governance at the Millennium: Where We Have Been - Where We Should Go", *Ocean & Coastal Management*, Vol 42 (1999).

Gattuso, Jr, J A and Tanner, L J, "Set and Drift: Naval Force in the New Century", *Naval War College Review*, Vol LIV, No 1 (Winter 2001).

Goold, M and Campbell, A, "Do You Have a Well-Designed Organisation?", *Harvard Business Review*, (Mar 2002).

Green, C and Penning-Rowsell, E, "Inherent Conflicts at the Coast", *Journal of Coastal Conservation*, Vol 5, Issue 2 (1999).

Gupta, M, Fletcher, S, "The Application of a Proposed Generic Institutional Framework for Integrated Coastal Management to India" *Ocean & Coastal Management*, Vol. 44 (2001).

Hatziolos, M E, "A World Bank Framework for Integrated Coastal Zone Management With Special Emphasis on Africa", *Ocean &d Coastal Management*, Vol. 37, No. 3 (1997).

Havens, J, "Terrorism; Ready to Blow", *Bulletin of the Atomic Scientists*, (Jul-Aug 2003).

Imperial, M T, "Analysing Institutional Arrangements for Ecosystem Based Management: Lessons from the Rhode Island Salt Ponds Plan", *Ocean & Coastal Management*, Vol. 27, No. 1 (1999).

J S Brown and P Duguid, "Organizational Learning and Communities-of-Practice; Toward a Unified View of Working, Learning and Innovation", *Organization Science*, Vol 2, No 1, 1991).

Jorge, M A, "Developing Capacity for Coastal Management in the Absence of the Government: A Case Study in the Dominican Republic", *Ocean &Coastal Management*, Vol 36, No 1-3 (1997).

Joseph, K A and Balchand, A N, "The Application of Coastal Regulation Zones in Coastal Management - Appraisal of Indian Experience", *Ocean & Coastal Management*, Vol 43, No 1 (2000).

Joyner, C C, "The International Ocean Regime at the New Millennium: A Survey of the Contemporary Legal Order", *Ocean & Coastal Management*, Vol 43 (2000).

Kaplan, R S and Norton, D P "The Balanced Scorecard - Measures that Drive Performance", *Harvard Business Review*, 70(1) (1996).

Kaplan, R S and Norton, D P, "Having Trouble With Your Strategy Then Map it", *Harvard Business Review*, (Sep-Oct 2000).

Kaplan, R S, and Norton, D P, "Leading Change With the Balanced Scorecard", *Financial Executive*, 17 (16), (2001).

Kenchington, R, "Tourism in Coastal and Marine Environment: A Recreational Perspective", *Ocean & Coastal Management*, Vol 19, No 1 (1993).

Kim, W C and Mauborgne, R, "Charting Your Company's Future", *Harvard Business Review*, (Jun 2002).

Kullenberg, G, "The Exclusive Economic Zone: Some Perspectives", *Ocean & Coastal Management*, Vol 42 (1999).

Lau, H C W, Wong, C W Y, Hui, I K, Pun, K F, "Design and Implementation of an Integrated Knowledge System", *Knowledge Based Systems*, Vol xx (2002).

Levy, J P, "A National Ocean Policy: An Elusive Quest", *Marine Policy*, Vol 17 No 2 (1993).

Lowry, K, "Federal-State Co-ordination in Coastal Management: An Assessment of the Federal Consistency Provision of the CZMA", *Ocean & Coastal Management*, Vol 19 No 2 (1993).

Luttinger, N, "Community-Based Coral Reef Conservation in the Bay and Islands of Honduras", *Ocean & Coastal Management*, Vol 36 No 1-3 (1997).

Mabudafhasi, R, "The Role of Knowledge Management and Information Sharing in Capacity Building for Sustainable Development-an Example from South Africa" *Ocean & Coastal Management*, Vol 45 (2002).

Mani, J S, "Report: Coastal Zone Management Plans and Policies in India", *Coastal Management*, Vol 25 No 1 (1997).

Marriott, S P, "Fisheries Institutional Reform in Developing Countries", *Marine Policy*, Vol 21, No 5 (1997).

McConnell, M., "Capacity Building for a Sustainable Shipping Industry: A Key Ingredient in Improving Coastal and Ocean and Management", *Ocean & Coastal Management*, Vol 45 (2002).

Mcintyre, A D, "Troubled Waters: The Future of the Oceans", *IAEA Bulletin*, 45/1 (2003).

McIntyre, O and Mosedale, T, "The Precautionary Principle as a Norm of Customary International Law", *Journal of Environmental Law*, Vol 9 No 2 (1997).

Miles, E L, "The Concept of Ocean Governance: Evolution Toward the 21st Century and the Principle of Sustainable Ocean Use", *Ocean & Coastal Management,* Vol 27, No 1 (1999).

Mitchell, C L, "Sustainable Ocean Development: The Canadian Approach", *Marine Policy,* Vol 24 No 4/5 (1998).

Nayak, B U, Chandramohan, P and Desai, B N, "Planning and Management of the Coastal Zone in India: A Perspective", *Coastal Management,* Vol 20 (1993).

Noble, B F, "Institutional Criteria for Co-management", *Marine Policy,* Vol 24 No 1 (2000).

Olsen, S and Christie P, "What are We Learning from Tropical Coastal Management Experience?", *Ocean & Coastal Management,* Vol 28 No 1 (2000).

Olsen, S, Tobey, J and Kerr, M, "A Common Framework for Learning from ICM Experience", *Ocean & Coastal Management,* Vol 37 No 2 (1997).

Parmente, D, "The Balanced Scorecard", *New Zealand Management,* Vol 49, Issue 4, (May 2002).

Pomeroy, R S, "Community-Based and Co-management Institutions for Sustainable Coastal Fisheries Management in Southeast Asia", *Ocean & Coastal Management,* Vol 27, No 3 (1995).

Rapha el Bill!e, R, Mermet, L, "Integrated Coastal Management at the Regional Level: Lessons from Toliary, Madagascar", *Ocean & Coastal Management,* Vol 45 (2002).

Rivera, R and New Kirk, G K, "Power of the People: A Documentation of Non-Governmental Organisations Experience in Community-Based Coastal Resource Management in the Philippines", *Ocean & Coastal Management,* Vol 36, No 1-3 (1997).

Salz, P, "Some Questions Regarding Problem Definition in Coastal Management Research", *Journal of Coastal Conservation,* Vol 5, Issue 2 (1999).

Simth, H D, "The Industrialisation of the World Ocean", *Ocean & Coastal Management,* Vol 44 (2001).

Singh, S, "Ocean Policy for India", *Journal of Indian Ocean Studies,* Vol 3, No 3 (1996).

Smith, H D, "The Industrialisation of the World Ocean", *Ocean & Coastal Management,* Vol 43, No 1 (2000).

Sorensen, J, "The International Proliferation of Integrated Coastal Zone Management Efforts", *Ocean & Coastal Management*, Vol 21 No 1-3 (1993).

Sorensen, J, "National and International Efforts at Integrated Coastal Management: Definitions, Achievements and Lessons", *Coastal Management*, No 25 (1997).

Steins, N A and Edwards, V M, "Institutional Analysis of UK Coastal Fisheries; Implications of Overlapping Regulations for Fisheries Management", *Marine Policy*, Vol 21, No 6 (1997).

Stenmark, D "Leveraging Tacit Organisational Knowledge", *Journal of Management Information Systems*, Vol 17, No 3 (Winter 2000-2001).

Sudara, S, "Who and What is to be Involved in Successful Coastal Zone Management: a Thailand Example", *Ocean & Coastal Management*, Vol 42 (1999).

Suman, S, "Case Studies of Coastal Conflicts: Comparative US/ European Experiences", *Ocean & Coastal Management*, Vol 44 (2001).

Ted L McDorman, T L, "Global Ocean Governance and International Adjudicative Dispute Resolution", *Ocean & Coastal Management*, Vol 43 (2000).

Thia-Eng, C, "Essential Elements of Integrated Coastal Zone Management', *Ocean & Coastal Management*, Vol 21 No 1-3 (1993).

Thia-Eng, C, Humming, Y and Guoqiang, C, "From Sectoral to Integrated Coastal Management: A Case in Xiamen, China", *Ocean & Coastal Management*, Vol 37, No 2 (1997).

Till, G, (2003). "Can Small Navies Stay Afloat", *Jane's Navy International* (May 2003).

Underdal, A, "Integrated Marine Policy: What? Where? How?", *Marine Policy* (Jul 1980).

Valencia, M J, "Energy and Insecurity in Asia", *Survival*, Vol 28, No 3 (Autumn 1997).

Vallega, A, "The Regional Scale of Ocean Management", *Ocean & Coastal Management*, Vol 39, No 3 (1998).

Vallejo, S M A, "The Integration of Coastal Zone Management into National Development Planning", *Ocean and Coastal Management*, Vol 21, No 1-3 (1993).

Visser, L, "The Socio-Institutional Dynamics of Coastal Zone Management", *Journal of Coastal Conservation*, Vol 5, Issue 2 (1999).

Wescott, G, "The Development and Initial Implementation of Australia's 'Integrated and Comprehensive' Oceans Policy", *Ocean & Coastal Management*, Vol 43 (2000).

## Reports

Biliana Cicin-Sain, Patricio Bernal, Veerle Vandeweerd, Stefano Belfiore, and Kevin Goldstein, A Guide to Oceans, Coasts, and Islands at the World Summit on Sustainable Development, Center for the Study of Marine Policy, Newark, Delaware, August 2002.

Carrillo, P M, Anumba, C J and Kamara, J M (2000), Knowledge Management Strategy for Construction: Key IT and Contextual Issues, Proceedings of CIT 2000, Reykjavik, Iceland, 28-30 June, Gudnason, G (ed), pp.155-165.

Clayton, B D and Bass, S, (2002), Recent progress and new thinking on Strategies for Sustainable Development. Paper presented at the Annual meeting of the International Association for Impact Assessment, 15-21 June 2002. Netherlands Congress Center, Hague.

Epstein, Marc and P Wisner (2001), Good Neighbours: Implementing Social and Environmental Strategies with the BSC. In Balanced Scorecard Report. May/June 2001, 3:3. Massachusetts: HBS Publishing.

Figge, Frank; Hahn, Tobias; Schaltegger, Stefan & Wagner, Marcus. (2001), Sustainability Balanced Scorecard. Center for Sustainability Management, Lüneburg 2001

Goldblat, J, (1992), Maritime Security: the Building of Confidence. UNDIR, New York.

Halle, M, Switzer, J and Winkler, S, (2002), Trade, Aid and Security: Elements of a Positive Paradigm - A Working Paper. International Institute for Sustainable Development (IISD) and IUCN - The World Conservation Union.

Hockerts, Kai (2001), Corporate Sustainability Management - Towards Controlling Corporate Ecological and Social Sustainability, In: Proceedings of Greening of Industry Network Conference, 21-24 January 2001, Bangkok.

Shankar, S, (2001), Measuring the Business Impact of Knowledge Management: A Conceptual Framework, Pennsylvania State University, 2001.

Sorensen, J (2002), Baseline 2000 Background Report: The Status of Integrated Coastal Management as an International Practice.

Urban Harbors Institute, University of Massachusetts, Boston.

http://www.uhi.umb.edu/b2k/index.htm

Tata Energy Research Institute (TERI), (2002), Defining an Integrated Energy Strategy for India: Ensuring Security, Sufficiency and Sustainability. TERI, New Delhi

Keshkamat, SS, (1999), "Present status and future plans for the development of tourism in Goa" Proceedings of the workshop on Integrated Coastal and Marine Area Management Plan for Goa. 25-26 August 1999.

Subramanian, B R, Vincent, D, (1999), Integrated Coastal and Marine Area Management Plan for Gulf of Kachchh - Concept, Processes and Application. Proceedings of the workshop on Integrated Coastal and Marine Area Management Plan for Gulf of Kachchh. 23-24 August 1999.

Ministry of Environment and Forests Orders S O 991 (E) to S O 1004 (E) of 26 November, 1998 and S O 577 (E) of 13 July 1999. Published by Authority in The Gazette of India.

Ninth Five Year Plan (1997-2002) Volume 1, Development Goals, Strategy and Policies. Planning Commission. Government of India.

Tenth Five Year Plan (1997-2002) Volume 1, Dimensions and Strategies. Planning Commission. Government of India.

Economic Survey 2002-2003. Ministry of Finance and Company Affairs Economic Division. Government of India.

Vision Perspective Plan 2015, Department of Ocean Development. Government of India.

National Tourism Policy 2002, Department of Tourism, Ministry of Tourism and Culture. Government of India.

Tourism Statistics 2001, Department of Tourism, Ministry of Tourism and Culture. Government of India.

Petroleum Exploration and Production Activities India 2002-03. Directorate General of Hydro Carbons. Ministry of Petroleum and Natural Gas. Government of India.

The Indian Hydrocarbon sector spreads its Wings. Ministry of Petroleum and Natural Gas. Government of India.

Basic Statistics on Indian Petroleum and Natural Gas 2002-03. Ministry of Petroleum and Natural Gas. Government of India.

Basic Ports Statistics of India 2000-2001. Ministry of Shipping. Government of India.

Annual Report 2002-2003. Ministry of Shipping. Government of India.

Update on Indian Port Sector (Upto 31 Mar 03). Ministry of Shipping. Government of India.

Annual Review 2003. Indian National Shipowner's Association.

Report of the Steering Committee on Environment, Forest and Wildlife for the Tenth Five Year Plan (2002-2007). Planning Commission. Government of India.

Report of the Working Group on Fisheries for the Tenth Five Year Plan (2002-2007). Planning Commission. Government of India.

Planning Commission of India, (2001). India as a Knowledge Superpower: Strategy for transformation. Planning Commission, New Delhi.

The Constitution of India 2000. Ministry of Law, Justice and Company Affairs. Government of India.

Ocean Governance: Towards an Oceanic Circle. UNDOALOS/ UNITAR Briefing on Developments in Ocean Affairs and the LOS - 20 years After the Conclusion of UNCLOS - UN-HQ, NY, September 25 & 26, 2002

United Nations Division for Ocean Affairs and the Law of the Sea (UNDOAL0S), (2002). Oceans: The Source of life. United Nations Convention on Law of the Sea, 20th Anniversary (1982 - 2002).

United Nations Educational Scientific and Cultural Organisation (UNESCO), (2002). One Planet, One Ocean - Sustainable Development of Oceans and Coasts: a Commitment of 129 States at Johannesburg 2002 IOC Information documents series No. 1172, UNESCO 2002

United Nations Economic and Social Council Report (UNESC), (2001). Commission on Sustainable Development acting as the preparatory Committee for the World Summit on Sustainable Development organisational session. Report of the Secretary General - Oceans and Seas.

United Nations Economic and Social Council (UNESC), (1997). Overall progress achieved since the UN conference on Environment and Development.

United Nations Economic and Social Council (UNESC), (2001). Report of the Ad Hoc open-ended Intergovernmental group of experts on Energy and Sustainable Development. 26 Feb - 02 March, 2001, New York.

United Nations Economic and Social Commission for Asia and the Pacific (UNESCAP)Study on the Regional Shipping and Port Development Strategies under a changing Maritime Environment using the ESCAP/UNDP Maritime Policy Planning Model.

Rio Declaration on Environment and Development(1992). United Nations Conference on Environment and Development (UNCED) Annexure 1, UN Document A/CONF.151/26 (Vol. I)

Report of the Secretary General - Integrating Environment and Development in decision-making.

International Union for Conservation of Natural Resources (IUCN), (2001). IUCN 2001 Global Programme Progress and Assessment Report.

IUCN Report on State-of-the-Art Review on Environment, Security and Development Co-operation For the Working Party on Development Co-operation and Environment. OECD Development Assistance Committee.

IWCO (Independent World Commission on the Ocean) (1998). The Ocean : Our Future. (ed M Soares), Cambridge.

WWF/IUCN Marine Policy. Creating a Sea Change.

WWF/IUCN (2001). The status of natural resources on the high-seas. WWF/IUCN, Gland, Switzerland.

Summary of the Discussion for the areas of focus: (a) the protection and preservation of the marine environment, and (b) capacity-building, regional cooperation and coordination and integrated ocean management. United Nations Open-ended Informal Consultative Process established by the General Assembly in its resolution 54/33 in order to facilitate the annual review by the Assembly of developments in ocean affairs; Third meeting (New York, 8-15 April 2002)

European Code of Conduct for Coastal Zones. (1999). Committee for the activities of the council of Europe in the field of Biological and landscape diversity. Secretariat General, Directorate of Environment and Local authorities.

European Commission Demonstration Programme (ECDP), (1999). Lessons from the European Commissions Demonstration Programme on Integrated Coastal Zone Management (ICZM). Programme on Integrated Management in Coastal Zones 1997-1999. Directorates-General Environment, Nuclear Safety and Civil Protection , Fisheries, Regional Policies and Cohesion.

Towards a European Integrated Coastal Zone Management (ICZM) Strategy: General Principles and Policy Options. (1999). European Commission Demonstration Programme on Integrated Management in Coastal Zones 1997-1999. Directorates-General Environment, Nuclear Safety and Civil Protection, Fisheries, Regional Policies and Cohesion.

World Development Report (WDR), (2002).Building Institutions for Markets. The World Bank, Washington DC.

World Development Report (WDR), (2003). Sustainable Development in a Dynamic World: transforming Institutions, Growth and Quality of Life. The World Bank and Oxford University Press: New York.

World Summit on Sustainable Development (WSSD), (2002). Plan for Implementation.

## Internet Sources

UNDOALOS - Full Text of the Law of the Sea http://www.un.org/Depts/los/convention_agreements/texts/unclos/closindx.htm

Earth Summit 1992 Agenda 21 - Full Text

http://www.un.org/esa/sustdev/documents/agenda21/english/agenda21toc.htm

The World Commission on Environment and the Development (WECD). "Our Common Future" The Brundtland Report 1987

http://ods-dds-ny.un.org/doc/UNDOC/GEN/N87/184/67/IMG/N8718467.pdf?OpenElement

Department of Ocean Development. http://www.nic.in/dod/dodhead.htm

Environmental Impact Assessment Division. Ministry of Environment and Forests. Government of India.

http://envfor.nic.in/divisions/iass/iass.htmlhttp://envfor.nic.in/divisions/iass/iass.html

Good Governance: The business of government (2000). India: Policies to reduce poverty and accelerate sustainable development. World

Bank. http://wbln1018.worldbank.org/sar/sa.nsf/Attachments/GoodGovernance/$File/chapt4.pdf

India Country Brief 99. World Bank Report.

http://wbln1018.worldbank.org/sar/sa.nsf/a22044d0c4877a3e852567de0052e0fa/bda6b892e28b548b852567ef005a0a85

India Country profile. Integrated Coastal Management: An International priority. http://icm.noaa.gov/country/india/india.html

India's Biodiversity. Tata Energy Research Institute Report.

http://www.teriin.org/biodiv/status.htm

National Institute Of Oceanography http://www.nio.org/projects/coastal7.htm

Onge, H S, (1995-1999). Knowledge Management. http://knowinc.com/saint-onge/primer/hso14.htm

Pernetta, J C (1993). Marine Protected Area Needs in the South Asian Seas Region Volume 2: India (online). Switzerland, IUCN, Gland. http://iucn.org/cgi-bin/byteserver.pl/themes/marine/pdf/mpan_v2.pdf

Project Directorate, ICMAM. http://linux.tn.nic.in/icmam/

SustainAbility: Strategic Management Consultancy and think tank (1987). http://www.sustainability.com/programs/Business_Case/default.asp

Union Government Ministries/Departments. National Information Centre. http://indiaimage.nic.in/ug.htm

Wells, S, Dwivedi, N, Singh, S, Ivan, R, (1998). Marine Region 10: Central Indian Ocean (online). A report to the World Bank Environment Department. http://www.environment.gov.au/library/pubs/mpa/chap10.html

SeaPlant Communities, 2002. - the Surialink concept - Geographic Information System. http://www.surialink.com/GIS/stats_summ.asp

Regional Seminar on Liberalization of Maritime Transport Services under WTO GATS 11 - 13 February 2002 Bangkok, Thailand, India Country Report. http://www.unescap.org/tctd/nvg/wtogats2002files/india_wtogats.pdf

Singh, H.S., (2002). Marine Protected Areas of India: Status of wetland conservation. http://www.iucn.org/themes/wcpa/newsbulletins/news/MPA_WCPAindia.pdf

Prime Minister of India's announcements on Independence Day, 2003 August 15, 2003 http://pmindia.nic.in/idas15aug2k3.pdf.

Barry Dalal-Clayton and Stephen Bass (2002). Sustainable Development Strategies: A Resource Book for Organisation for Economic Cooperation and Development and United Nations Development Programmme.

http://www.nssd.net/working/resource/indexa.htm

High Performance Systems - Ithink software is a simple yet powerful tool for building better models, simulating them more reliably, and communicating them more effectively. With ithink, it's possible to create models that truly have impact - changing minds and changing behavior in ways that result in sustainable improvements in business performance. http://www.hps-inc.com

## Newspapers

"US. UK ships caught snooping in Indian waters", Times of India (New Delhi), 01 February 2001.

"Norms proposed for implementing Sagar Mala programme", The Hindu (Online edition), 21 September 2003.

"Cess for Sagar Mala: Enabling law mooted", The Hindu (Business Line), 8 November 2003.

"Draft outline of Sagar Mala project - Forging strong links in the transport chain", The Hindu (Business Line), 10 November 2003.

"Strategic Oil storage plan gets the nod", Indian Express (New Delhi), 08 January 2004.

"Crude reserves to be set up", The Hindu (New Delhi), 08 January 2004.

"Cabinet okays 23 SeZs, strategic oil reserves", Hindustan Times (New Delhi), 08 January 2004.

"Power Politics & Pipe(line) dreams: India need gas, but diplomacy will drive three trans-Asian proposals", The Times of India (New Delhi), 12 January 2004.

"Environment policy draft to be ready soon", The Hindu (New Delhi), 21 January 2004.

"Change Environment laws", The Hindu (New Delhi), 22 January 2004.

"Oil cess planned to fund strategic reserves", The Hindu (New Delhi), 22 January 2004.

# Index